SELECTED WORKS OF HENRY JAMES, SR.—4

MORALISM AND CHRISTIANITY

AMS PRESS

NEW YORK

MORALISM AND CHRISTIANITY;

OR

Man's Experience and Destiny.

IN THREE LECTURES,

BY

HENRY JAMES.

NEW-YORK:

J. S. REDFIELD.

———

1850

Library of Congress Cataloging in Publication Data

James, Henry, 1811–1882.
  Moralism and Christianity.

  (Selected works of Henry James, Sr.)
  Reprint. Originally published: New York: J.S. Redfield, 1850.
  1. Christianity—Addresses, essays, lectures.
I. Title. II. Series: James, Henry, 1811–1882.
Selections. 1983.
BR123.J35   1983   201   72-917
ISBN 0-404-10084-8

AMS PRESS, INC.
56 East 13th Street, New York, N.Y. 10003

Reprinted from the edition of 1850, New York. Trim size has been
slightly altered. Original trim: 10.7 × 18.6 cm.

INTERNATIONAL STANDARD BOOK NUMBER
Complete set: 0-404-10080-5
Vol. 4: 0-404-10084-8

MANUFACTURED
IN THE UNITED STATES OF AMERICA

ADVERTISEMENT.

THE first of the three following Lectures, after its delivery in New-York, was put in its present form for publication in the " MASSACHUSETTS QUARTERLY REVIEW," whence it is now re-published with a few verbal emendations. The second Lecture was read Nov. 1, 1849, before the TOWN AND COUNTRY CLUB, Boston, and is here slightly enlarged. The third Lecture was read, and subsequently repeated at the request of several gentlemen, in New-York during the month of December, 1849. It has been greatly enlarged for publication. The topics are perhaps somewhat difficult from their novelty, and if therefore the writer should appear to have treated them inadequately, he doubts not that the generous reader will allow this circumstance its due force in mitigation of judgment.

CONTENTS.

A SCIENTIFIC STATEMENT

DOCTRINE OF THE LORD.

~~~~~~~~~~~

THE Christian doctrine of the Lord, or Divine Man, rests upon this fundamental axiom, that God alone is being, or life in Himself. Man is not being, but only a subject of being, only a form or image of being. His being is not absolute, but phenomenal, as conditioned in space and time. But God's being is utterly unconditioned either in space or time. It is infinite, not as comprehending all space, but as utterly excluding the bare conception of space ; and eternal, not as comprehending all time, but as utterly excluding the bare conception of time. He is not a subject of being, but being itself, and therefore the sole being.

Consistently with this fundamental axiom, we are bound to deny that the creature of God has any being or substance in himself. The substantial being or life of every creature is God, while the creature is but a form or image of God. The creature is not another being than God, nor yet is he an identical being with God ; because the creature is not being at all, but only a shadow or reflection of being.   You would not call the shadow of the tree on the ground another substance than the tree itself, nor yet the same substance, for the reason that the shadow is not any substance at all, but merely the image of a substance.   So man, the shadow or image of God, is neither a different being from God, nor yet an identical being, because he is not any being whatever, but only the reflection of being. Thus God's creature is without any being or substance in himself, his selfhood being nothing more than an image or reflection of the only and universal being, which is God.   The internal of every man is God.   The external, or that which defines the man, defines his self-consciousness, is only a shadow or reflection of this internal.

These things being granted, which they must be as it seems to the writer, unless one prefers to deny the fact of creation, it follows from them that the universe of creation is a vast theatre of imagery or correspondence.   If God be the sole and therefore universal being, his universal creature can be nothing more and nothing less than His image or shadow.   And if the creature be only the image or

shadow of God, then creation itself is not the origi-
nation of any new being or substance on the part of
God, but only the revelation or imaging forth of a
being which is eternal and unchangeable. Thus in
the light of the principles here stated, the created
universe resolves itself both in whole and in part
into an imagery or correspondence of God, and the
universal science consequently, or the science of
sciences, becomes the science of correspondence.

If now all this be true, if it be true that creation can be nothing more and nothing less than the
revealing or imaging forth of God, then some mo-
mentous results immediately ensue to our theology
and philosophy. Primarily it results that the true
creature of God is not finite, cannot be compre-
hended within the laws of space and time. For as
the creature is only an image or reflection of God,
and as God being eternal and infinite is utterly ignorant both of time and space, so His true creature
cannot be finited by these conditions. Thus the life
of nature, or that life which lies within the laws of
space and time, does not image God. The only
life which does image Him consequently is one that
transcends these laws, being a spiritual life, and
this life belongs exclusively to man.

But in order to justify this affirmation, it is necessary to state what we mean by spirit as distinguished from sensible nature. In speaking of the spirit of a thing in contradistinction to the sensible thing itself, nothing else is meant than its distinctive genius, or faculty of operation. For example, the horse is an outward form discernible by my senses from all other natural forms. But there is something more in the horse than meets my eye, namely, a certain faculty or capacity of use, which constitutes his distinctive spirit or genius, and is cognizable only by the eye of my understanding. Thus what is spiritual about the horse is what lies within his material form, and constitutes his power or faculty of use. This faculty is different in the horse from what it is in every other animal, the cow, the sheep, the ox, the lion, the elephant, etc. Take another example from the sphere of the arts. My hat is an artificial form sensibly distinct from all other forms. But this outward or sensible form of the hat does not exist by itself. It embodies a certain use or function, namely the protection of my head, which use or function constitutes its spirit. In short the spirit of a thing is the end or use for which it exists. Thus you may take the whole range either of nature or the arts, and you will find everything existing for a certain use beyond itself,

which use is the spiritual ground or justification of
its existence. Nature is properly nothing more than
the robe or garment of spirit. It is only the tabernacle or house of spirit, only the subservient instrument or means by which spirit subsists and becomes conscious. Every thing in nature, without
any the most insignificant exception, embodies an
internal use or capacity of operation, which constitutes its peculiar spirit. Deprive it of this internal
use or capacity, not only actually or for a limited
time, but potentially or for ever, and you deprive it
of life. Exhaust the power of the horse to bear a
burden and draw a load, of the cow to produce milk,
of the sheep to produce wool, of the tree to produce
fruit or seed, and you at the same time consign them
all to death. For death, or the departure of the
spirit from the body, means in every case the cessation of the subject's capacity of use. Thus nature in all its departments is merely the vehicle or
minister of spirit. Its true sphere is that of entire
subjection to spirit, and never since the world began
has an instance occurred of its failing to exhibit the
most complete acquiescence in this subjection.

But if this spiritual force reside in Nature, what
hinders any natural form being a true revelation or
image of God ? If, for example, the horse possess a

spiritual substratum, why does not the horse image
God ?   The reason is obvious.   The spirit of the
horse is not his own spirit.   He is entirely unconscious of it.   He performs incessant uses to man,
but does not perform them *of himself*.   His end is
external to himself.   The object of his actions does
not fall within his own subjectivity.   The spirit of
universal nature is a spirit of subjection to some external power.   It never manifests itself spontaneously, but always in obeisance to some outward
constraint.   Thus the horse does not spontaneously
place himself in the harness.   The cow does not
come to your dairy, to make a spontaneous surrender of her milk.   The sheep feels no spontaneous
impulsion to deposit his fleece at your door.   Nor
does the tree inwardly shake itself in order to supply you with apples.   In short there is no such
thing as a spiritual horse—cow—sheep—or apple
tree.

> Sic vos non vobis nidificatis aves,
> Sic vos non vobis vellera fertis oves,
> Sic vos non vobis mellificatis apes,
> Sic vos non vobis fertis aratra boves.

No, all these performances are for the benefit of
man.   The whole realm of nature is destitute of a
spiritual consciousness, of such a consciousness as

elevates any of its forms to the dignity of a person. No animal is conscious of a self hood distinct from its outward or natural limitations. No animal is capable of suicide, or the renunciation of its outer life, on the ground of its no longer fulfilling the aspiration of its inner life. Thus nature is destitute of any proper personality. The only personality it recognizes is man. To him all its uses tend. Him all its powers obey. To his endowment and supremacy it willingly surrenders itself, and finds life in the surrender. Take away man accordingly, and nature remains a clod, utterly spiritless—impersonal—dead.

Thus nature does not image or reveal God. For God's activity is not imposed. It is spontaneous, or self-generated. It flows from Himself exclusively, and ignores all outward motive. Hence God's true creature or image is bound above all things to exhibit that power of self-derived or spontaneous action which constitutes our idea of the divine personality.

Accordingly it is man alone who fulfills this requisition. Man alone possesses personality, or the power of self-derived action. Personality, the quality of being a person, means simply the power of self-derived or supernatural action, the power of

originating one's own action, or, what is the same
thing, of acting according to one's own sovereign
pleasure. It means a power of acting unlimited by
any thing but the will of the subject. Thus, in as-
cribing personality to God, we do not mean to assert
for him certain bodily limitations palpable to sense,
which would be absurd ; we mean merely to assert
His self-sufficiency or infinitude—His power to act
according to his own sovereign pleasure. We
mean, in plain English, to assert that He is the exclusive source of His own actions. So also, in as-
cribing personality to man and denying it to the
horse, we mean to assert that man possesses the
power of supernatural or infinite action, the power
of acting independently of all natural constraint, and
according to his own individual or private attract-
tion, while the horse has not this power. Man's
action, when it is truly personal, has its source in
himself, in his own private tastes or attractions, as
contra-distinguished on the one hand from his physical necessities, and on the other from his social
obligations ; therefore we affirm man's personality,
or his absolute property in his actions. Nature's
action has not its source in any interior self, but in
some outward and constraining power ; therefore
we deny nature any personality, any absolute pro-

perty in its actions. When the fire burns my
incautious finger, I do not blame the fire, and why?
Because I feel that the fire acts in strict obedience
to its nature, which is that of subjection to me, and
that I alone have been in fault, therefore, for re-
versing this relation and foolishly subjecting myself
to it.

But now, if personality imply the power of self-
derived or spontaneous action, then it is manifest
that this power supposes in the subject a composite
self-hood. It supposes its subject to possess an internal or spiritual self as the end or object of the action, and an external or natural self as its means or
instrument. For clearly, when you attribute any
action to me personally, or affirm my exclusive property in it, you do not mean to affirm that it was
prompted by my nature, that nature which is common to me and all other men, but by my private
taste or inclination. You hold that I have some internal end, some private object to gratify by it, and
thereupon you declare the action mine. I repeat,
then, that personality, or the power of self-derived
action, supposes a dual or composite selfhood in the
subject, a selfhood composed of two elements, one
internal, spiritual, or private, the other external,
natural, or public.

But this is not all. Personality, or the power of self-derived action, not only supposes this composite selfhood in the subject, not only supposes him to possess an internal self, and an external self, but it also supposes that these two shall be perfectly united in every action which is properly called his. For example, I perform a certain action which you pronounce mine, on the ground of its having visibly proceeded from my hand. Now I say, this is not sufficient to prove the action absolutely mine. In order to prove it absolutely mine, you must not only show that it was done by my hand or my external self, but also that this external self did not at the time dominate or overrule my internal self. If the two elements of my personality were not perfectly united, perfectly concurrent, in the action; if the internal self were overruled by the external, or *vice versa;* then the action is not truly mine, is not a legitimate progeny of my will and understanding, but a bastard or *filius nullius*, abhorred of God and man.

Let me precisely illustrate my meaning by a case in point. A certain man is murdered by me. You witness the deed and denounce me as the murderer. On my trial it is proved that the deceased stood in the way of a certain inheritance coming to me;

that I had exhibited various marks of vexation at
this circumstance, and had been heard to wish him
out of the way, and even threaten to remove him
myself. Your direct testimony, backed by such
evidence as to my state of mind with regard to the
deceased, leaves no doubt as to my actual guilt. I
am accordingly convicted and hanged. For all that
the community wants to know is, which of its members actually committed the deed, that knowing
this they may proceed to avenge it. The care of
the state extends only to the outward or public life
of its members, not to their inner or private interests. In making inquisition into the murder, it has
no desire to decide as to my interior or spiritual condition ; this it leaves to God, who sees the heart. It
only seeks to know the actual perpetrator, that it
may not punish the innocent for the guilty. Thus,
in pronouncing the murderous deed mine, it does
not mean to say that it pertains to me spiritually,
but only outwardly or visibly ; pertains to me,
A. B., as outwardly distinguished from C. D., E. F.,
and the rest. To outward view, then, or in man's
sight, the action is doubtless mine, and I submit
my body to man's law. But now, admitting the
deed to be thus far mine, admitting that I actually
slew the man, and am therefore responsible to the

extent of my natural life ; is this deed necessarily mine to inward view also, or in God's sight?

I unhesitatingly say, No, and for this reason, that my internal or spiritual self and my external or natural self, did not really *unite* in it, but the former was overruled by the latter ?   How " overruled ?" I will show you.

Suppose me very much to dislike living in Germany, or any other of the old European states. The language, the manners, and the customs of the country, are all foreign to my habit, and I do not spontaneously make my abode in it.   But I am poor, with very few resources against natural want, and I hear of a fortune being left me in Germany, on condition of my going there to reside.   I accordingly go.   Now in this case my private or spiritual repugnance to this step was overruled by my natural necessities.   If I had enjoyed an ample supply of these necessities, I should not have gone.   My spiritual aversion to the step would not have allowed it.   But I was absolutely destitute of provision for my natural wants, save at the expense of abject toil, which a man hates, and it was this outward or natural destitution, which constrained my spirit into obedience.   Thus my spirit was overruled or dominated by my flesh, and the result consequently is that though to outward appearance or in man's sight I am in Germany, yet in reality or in God's sight I am still in America—that though my body is in Germany, my spirit is a thousand leagues away.

This example illustrates what I mean by "over-ruling" in the case of the murder. I say that the action in this case, though apparently mine or mine in man's sight, as having been performed by my hand, was yet not really or spiritually mine, was not mine in God's sight, because in doing it my spirit was overruled by my nature, and did not yield a spontaneous concurrence. I desired a certain inheritance capable of relieving me from pressing natural want. The longer I felt the want, the more urgent grew my desire for that which would relieve it, until at last it overcame my internal or spiritual repugnance to murder so far as to allow me to slay him, who alone stood in the way of its gratification. I am not attempting to palliate the enormity of the act. It is perfectly detestable in itself, and will always be so. I merely deny that my spirit and my flesh were *one* in it, which unity is necessary in every act that is spiritually mine. I merely assert that my spirit was *overruled* by my flesh to do this evil thing. The flesh gathering potency from want, from actual destitution, overruled or con-

strained the spirit to its ends, and the action consequently, instead of being really or spiritually mine,
is referable exclusively to what the theologians call
a *depraved nature*, meaning thereby a nature dis-
united or inharmonic with spirit. The universal
heart of man ratifies this judgment, or acquits me
spiritually of the deed, when it commends me to the
mercy of God. You have forfeited man's mercy,
say they; betake yourself, therefore, to that of God,
which is infinite, or open to all degrees of defilement.

No one dares forbid me, all red as I am with my
brother's blood, from hoping in God. This is a fact
full of meaning. The meaning of it is that we do not
believe any man to be evil at bottom or in his inmost heart, but only from a lack of outward freedom.
The meaning of it is that we consider none of our
judgments final, since they extend only to appearances, but look to have them overruled and correct-
ed by Him who sees the inmost heart, and judges
therefore according to the reality. A divine instinct,
in truth, in every soul of man, continually derides
all our criminality as transient or unreal, so that no
criminal ever shows himself so black as to make us
feel that he is beyond God's power to bless. No
man does evil save from the stress of nature or so-

ciety, save from a false position with respect to his own body or to his fellow-man. Accordingly we never hesitate to consign the worst of criminals to the boundless clemency of God. If we really believed the man to be bad in himself, bad independently of his physical and social conditions, we should never dare send him to God. We should do all in our power to hide him from God, as from a devouring pestilence.

Here let us pause a moment to survey the ground we have traversed. We have seen that creation is but the revelation or imaging forth of the divine personality. We have consequently seen that nature is incompetent to this revelation, because nature is destitute of personality, destitute of power to originate its own action. And finally we have seen that man is the only competent revelation or image of God, because man alone possesses personality. So far we have attained.

But now, from the definition given of personality, it is manifest that it is to be ascribed to man only in his very inmost or highest development, and not at all in his physical or social relations. For personality, when applied to any subject, affirms the subject's infinitude or perfection, affirms, in other words, the subject's entire sufficiency unto himself. It affirms his self-sufficiency or perfection, because it implies the power of originating his own action. He who has power to originate his own action is sufficient unto himself, and to be sufficient unto oneself is to be infinite or perfect. Infinitude or perfection means self-sufficiency. I admit the words are often used by rote, or without any definite intention. But whenever they are used intelligently, they are designed to express the subject's self-sufficiency. We can form no conception of the divine infinitude or perfection other than is expressed by saying that He is sufficient unto Himself. And if we further ask ourselves what we mean by His being sufficient unto Himself, we reply instinctively that we mean to express His power to originate his own action. This power, which is inherent in God, is the basis of His personality or character, is that thing, without which to our conception He would not be God, that is, would not be infinite or perfect. Had He not this power He would be finite or imperfect. His power, like that of nature, would be limited by something external to Himself.

If, therefore, personality, when applied to any subject, expresses his infinitude or perfection, expresses his self-sufficiency, it is manifest as was said before, that it cannot be applied to man in every aspect of his subjectivity, namely, as a subject either of nature or of his fellow-man, but only in his very highest aspect, which is that of a divine subject. For man's highest or inmost subjection is a subjection to God, which lifts him entirely beyond the sphere of necessity or duty, and indeed enables him, if need be, to lay off the bodily life and the friendship of men as easily as he lays off his garments at night. This subjection of man to God is involved in the very relation of Creator and creature. For the Creator being essential life, life in itself, cannot communicate life, save by communicating Himself to the creature. And He cannot communicate Himself, save in so far as the creature be made receptive, which receptivity becomes effected by means of the creature's natural and moral experience, the issue of which is to exalt him above nature and above society, endowing him with the lordship or supremacy of the external universe. Man's natural activity degrades or obscures his personality. It is not spontaneous—does not originate in his internal self, but in a mere necessity of his nature common to all its partakers. Instead of expressing his distinctive personality, therefore, it expresses a common property of all men. Regarded as a subject of nature, therefore, man lacks personality, lacks at least all such personality as reflects the divine.

His moral subjectivity presents a similar fatal defect. Morality covers my relations to society or my fellow-man. Thus, as my natural action is conditioned upon a law of necessity, or of subjection to nature, so my moral action is conditioned upon a law of duty, or of subjection to my fellow-man. I act morally only in so far as I act under obligation to others, being morally good when I practically acknowledge, and morally evil when I practically deny, this obligation. Thus morality displays me in subjection not to God, but to society or my fellow-man, and thus equally with nature denies me proper personality. For personality implies the subject's absolute property in his action, which property is impossible unless the subject constitute also the object of the action, or, in other words, unless the object of the action fall *within*, be internal to, the subject's self, and this condition is violated when I act not to please myself, but to please my fellow-man. Hence neither man's natural nor his moral action confers a divine or perfect personality on him. The former does not, because it displays him in subjection to nature. The latter does not, because it displays him in subjection to his fellow-man. Both the moral and natural man are imperfect. Both fail to exhibit that balanced or self-centred action, which is the exclusive basis of personality, and both alike consequently fail to express the DIVINE MAN, or accomplish the divine image in humanity.

But here it may be asked whether benevolence does not confer personality. Decidedly not, for the reason that benevolent action is not spontaneous but purely sympathetic. Personal action—all action which warrants the ascription of personality to the subject—is of necessity spontaneous, or inwardly begotten. I say of necessity, because action which is outwardly begotten, or originates in something foreign to the subject, does not pertain to him absolutely but only partially, pertains to him only as he stands involved in nature or society. Now sympathetic action evidently falls under this latter category, being begotten not from within but from without the subject's self, as the etymology of the word indicates. It supposes a want on the part of somebody not the subject, disposing the latter to relieve it. If, therefore, you take away suffering from all others, you take from the benevolent subject all power of action. And surely no one will consider that as a divine or perfect personality, whose power of action is controlled by circumstances foreign to itself.

Thus the fundamental requisite of personality,

namely, that it attest the subject's self-sufficiency or perfection by exhibiting in him the power of self-derived action, is necessarily made void in all purely benevolent action. And the inevitable conclusion therefore is, that the benevolent man, as such, does not possess true personality, or is incompetent to image God.

Who, then, *is* the true divine man? Who of all mankind possesses personality, and thus constitutes the image of God in creation? Evidently it must be some one who unites in himself, or harmonizes, all these finite or imperfect men. For the divine man does not exclude the natural man, nor the moral man, nor the sympathetic man, nor any other phasis of humanity. These are all constituent elements of the human nature, and the perfect man is bound not to exclude but accept them, blending and reconciling all in his own infinite manhood, in his own unitary self. These men are the geometric stones of the divine edifice of humanity ; they are by no means the edifice itself, but its indispensable *material*, and he therefore who should attempt to construct the edifice to their exclusion, would necessarily have his work about his ears.

Who, then, is the perfect or divine man, the man who actually reconciles in himself all the conflicting

elements of humanity ?   Is any such man actually
extant?   If so, where shall we find him?

We find him in the æsthetic man, or Artist.   But
now observe that when I speak of the æsthetic man
or Artist, I do not mean the man of any specific
function, as the poet, painter, or musician.   I mean
the man of whatsoever function, who in fulfilling it
obeys his own inspiration or taste, uncontrolled either by his physical necessities or his social obligations.   He alone is the Artist, whatever be his manifest vocation, whose action obeys his own internal
taste or attraction, uncontrolled either by necessity
or duty.   The action may perfectly consist both
with necessity and duty ; that is to say, it may
practically promote both his physical and social
welfare ; but these must not be its animating principles, or he sinks at once from the Artist into the
artisan.   The artisan seeks to gain a livelihood or
secure an honorable name.   He works for bread,
or for fame, or for both together.   The Artist abhors
these ends, and works only to show forth that immortal beauty whose presence constitutes his inmost
soul.   He is vowed to Beauty as the bride is vowed
to the husband, and beauty reveals herself to him
only as he is true to his inmost soul, only as he
obeys his spontaneous taste or attraction.

The reason accordingly why the painter, the poet, the musician, and so forth, have so long monopolized the name of Artist, is, not because Art is identical with these forms of action, for it is identical with no specific forms, but simply because the poet, painter, and so forth, more than any other men, have thrown off the tyranny of nature and custom, and followed the inspirations of genius, the inspirations of beauty, in their own souls. These men to some extent have sunk the service of nature and society in the obedience of their own private attractions. They have merged the search of the good and the true in that of the beautiful, and have consequently announced a divinity as yet unannounced either in nature or society. To the extent of their consecration, they are priests after the order of Melchisedec, that is to say, a priesthood, which, not being made after the law of a carnal commandment, shall never pass away. And they are kings, who reign by a *direct* unction from the Highest. But the priest is not the altar, but the servant of the altar; and the king is not the Highest, but the servant of the Highest. So painting, poetry, is not Art, but the servant and representative of Art. Art is divine, universal, infinite. It therefore exacts to itself infinite forms or manifestations, here

in the painter, there in the actor ; here in the musician, there in the machinist; here in the architect,
there in the dancer ; here in the poet, there in the
costumer. We do not therefore call the painter or
poet, Artist, because painting or poetry is a whit
more essential to Art than ditching is, but simply
because the painter and poet have more frequently
exhibited the life of Art by means of a hearty insubjection to nature and convention.

When, therefore, I call the divine man, or God's
image in creation, by the name of Artist, the reader
will not suppose me to mean the poet, painter, or
any other special form of man. On the contrary,
he will suppose me to mean that infinite and spiritual man whom all these finite functionaries represent indeed, but whom none of them constitutes,
namely, the man who in every visible form of action
acts always from his inmost self, or from attraction,
and not from necessity or duty. I mean the man
who is a law unto himself, and ignores all outward allegiance, whether to nature or society. This man
may indeed have no technical vocation whatever,
such as poet, painter, and the like, and yet he will
be none the less sure to announce himself. The
humblest theatre of action furnishes him a platform.
I pay my waiter so much a day for putting my din-

ner on the table. But he performs his function in a way so entirely *sui generis*, with so exquisite an attention to beauty in all the details of the service, with so symmetrical an arrangement of the dishes, and so even an adjustment of every thing to its own place, and to the hand that needs it, as to shed an almost epic dignity upon the repast, and convert one's habitual " grace before meat" into a spontaneous tribute, instinct with a divine recognition.

The charm in this case is not that the dinner is all before me, where the man is bound by his wages to place it. This every waiter I have had has done just as punctually as this man. No, it is exclusively the way in which it is set before me, a way altogether peculiar to this man, which attests that in doing it he is not thinking either of earning his wages, or doing his duty towards me, but only of satisfying his own conception of beauty with the resources before him. The consequence is that the pecuniary relation between us merges in a higher one. He is no longer the menial, but my equal or superior, so that I have felt, when entertaining doctors of divinity and law, and discoursing about divine mysteries, that a living epistle was circulating behind our backs, and quietly ministering to our wants, far more apocalyptic to an enlightened eye than any yet contained in books.

The reader may deem the illustration beneath the dignity of the subject. The more the pity for him in that case, since it is evident that his eyes have been fixed upon the shows of things, rather than upon the enduring substance. It is not indeed a dignified thing to wait upon tables. There is no dignity in any labor which is constrained by one's necessities. But still no function exists so abject or servile as utterly to quench the divine or personal element in it. It will make itself manifest in all of them, endowing them all with an immortal grace, and redeeming the subject from the dominion of mere nature and custom.

But whether the illustration be mean or not, it is fully to the point. The divine life in every man, the life which is the direct inspiration of God, and therefore exactly images God, consists in the obedience of one's own taste or attraction, where one's taste or attraction is uncontrolled by necessity or duty, by nature or society. I know that this definition will not commend itself to the inattentive reader. But let me leave my meaning fully expressed. I say, then, that I act divinely, or that my action is perfect, only when I follow my own taste or attraction, uncontrolled either by my natural wants or my obligations to other men. I do not mean that I act divinely when I follow my attractions to the denial of my physical wants and my social obligations ; but only in independence of them. If these things control my action, it will not be divine.

For example, I have what is ordinarily called a great love of luxury. That is, I have a spontaneous desire after all manner of exquisite accommodation for my body. I desire a commodious and beautiful house, graceful and expressive furniture, carriages and horses, and all the other appliances of easy living. But I lack the actual possession of all these things. I am utterly destitute of means to procure them. Yet my inextinguishable love for them prompts me incessantly to action. Now you perceive that my action in this case, being shaped or controlled by my want of all these things, cannot be free or spontaneous, cannot be divine as expressing myself alone. It will in fact be thoroughly servile. It will be abject toil instead of free action. That is, I shall probably begin by some low manual occupation, such as sawing wood or porterage. I shall diligently hoard every penny accruing from my occupation not necessary to my subsistence, that I may in time arise to a more commanding vocation, in which I may realize larger

gains, and so on until I shall have at length attained
my wishes, and achieved the necessary basis of my
personality.   This action, then, is completely undivine ; it does not originate in myself as disen-
gaged from nature and my fellow-man, but in myself as still involved in subjection to them, and burn-
ing to become free.   So long as this condition of
bondage lasts, you may be sure that my action will
be the action of a slave, and that the deference I pay
to morality will be purely prudential.   If the great
end, which is my personal emancipation, can be
better secured by strict attention to its maxims, of
course I shall observe them.   But if not, I
shall be likely to use *meum* and *tuum* quite indiffer-
ently, feeling, as the children of Israel felt on the
eve of their emancipation from Egypt, that the spoils
of the oppressor are divinely due to the oppressed.

But now, on the other hand, suppose my emancipation accomplished ; suppose me in possession of
all natural good, and of all social privileges ; suppose, in a word, that I am no longer in bondage to
nature or society, having secured ample wealth and
reputation, and become free, therefore, to act according to my own sovereign taste ; then you perceive, at a glance, that this love of luxury in my
bosom, instead of leading me merely to the accu-

mulation of wealth, would prompt me exclusively
to creative action, or a mode of action which would
enrich the community as much as myself. For,
having now all that nature and society yielded for
the satisfaction of this love, the love would not thereupon become extinct or satiated ; on the contrary,
it would burn all the brighter for the nourishment
it had received, and impel me, therefore, to new
and untried methods of gratifying it. Thus, instead of a mere absorbent or consumer, which my
natural and social destitution rendered me, I should
now become an actual producer of new wealth ; a
producer, too, whose power would be as infinite as
the love which inspired it was infinite, being derived from the infinite God Himself.

A man, then, does not truly act at all, does not
act in any such sense that the action may be pro-
nounced absolutely *his*, so long as his personality
remains undeveloped ; so long as he remains in
bondage to nature or society. Before he can truly
act or show forth the divine power within him, he
must be in a condition of perfect outward freedom,
of perfect insubjection to nature and society ; all his
natural wants must be supplied, and all social ad-
vantages must be open to him. Until these things
are achieved his action must be more or less imper-

fect and base. You may, indeed, frighten him into some show of decorum, by representations of God as an infallible policeman intent always on evil-doers, but success in this way is very partial. The church itself, in fact, which authorizes these representations, incessantly defeats their force by its doctrine of absolution, or its proclamation of mercy to the most successful villany, if only repentant at the last gasp. Not only the church, but the whole current of vital action defeats these safeguards. Thus our entire system of trade, as based upon what is called " unlimited competition," is a system of rapacity and robbery. A successful merchant like Mr. A. or B., is established only on the ruins of a thousand unsuccessful ones. Mr. A. or B. is not to be blamed individually. His heart is destitute of the least ill-will towards the men whom, perhaps, he has never seen, but whom he is yet systematically strangling. He acts in the very best manner society allows to one of his temper or genius. He feels an unmistakably divine aspiration after unlimited power ; a power, that is, which shall be unlimited by any outward impediment, being limited only by his own interior taste or attraction. He will seek the gratification of this instinct by any means the constitution of society ordains ; thus, by the utter destruction of every rival merchant, if society allows it.

So much for Mr. A. or B. regarded as in subjection to nature and society, or as still seeking a field for his personality.   But this is not the final and divine Mr. A. or B.   The final and divine Mr. A. or B. will have subjected both nature and society to himself, and will then exhibit, by virtue of that very force in him, which is now so destructively operative, a personality of unmixed benignity to every one. The voice of God, as declared in his present instincts after unlimited power, bids him, as it bade the Israelites of old, to spoil the oppressor, to cleave down every thing that stands in the way of his inheritance : suppose him once established in that good land which flows with milk and honey, and which God has surely promised him, and you will immediately find the same instinct manifested in measureless and universal benediction.

The Artist, then, is the Divine Man,—the only adequate image of God in nature,—because he alone acts of himself, or finds the object of his action always *within* his own subjectivity.   He is that true creature and son of God, whom God pronounces very good, and endows with the lordship of the whole earth.   It would not be difficult, in the wri-

ters's estimation, to show the reason why the evo-
lution of this man has required the whole past physical and moral experience of the race, nor yet to
show how perfectly he justifies all the historic features of Christianity, standing symbolized under
every fact recorded in the four gospels concerning
the Lord Jesus Christ. In some other place, or at
least on some future occasion, the writer will un-
dertake these tasks.

SOCIALISM AND CIVILIZATION,

IN RELATION

TO THE DEVELOPMENT OF THE

INDIVIDUAL LIFE.

3*

LECTURE.

~~~~~~~~~

GENTLEMEN:

I propose to discuss the relative bearing of Socialism and Civilization on human destiny, or the development of the individual life.

By Socialism, I mean not any special system of social organization, like that of Fourier, Owen, or St. Simon, but what is common to all these systems, namely, the idea of a perfect fellowship or society among men. And by Civilization, of course, I mean the present political constitution of the nations. Between the fundamental idea of Socialism, which affirms the possibility of a perfect life on earth, or the insubjection of man both to nature and his fellow-man, and the fundamental idea of Civilization, which affirms the perpetual imperfection of human life, or the permanent subjection of man to nature and society, a great discrepancy exists; and I hope to interest my audience in a brief examination of its features. I am sure you cannot bestow your spontaneous attention upon the subject without the greatest advantage.

The differences of detail which characterize the systems of St. Simon, Owen, Fourier, and other societary reformers, are of very little present account to us. What is of great present account is the signal agreement of these men in point of principle. They agree in holding our present social condition to be not only vicious, which every one will admit, but also stupid, which is not so universally obvious. They declare that it is entirely competent to us at any time to organize relations of profound and enduring harmony among men, and thus to banish crime, vice, and suffering from the earth; and that nothing but an ignorance of the true principles of human nature stands between us and this most desirable consummation. Crime, vice and suffering, they allege, are not essential to human society, but are merely incidental to its infancy or nonage, and are sure to disappear before the advancing wisdom of its majority. Thus the socialist maintains the inherent righteousness of humanity, and resolves all its disorders into imperfect science.

Here, then, we have the fundamental difference between Socialism and Civilization. The socialist affirms the inherent righteousness of humanity, affirms that man is sufficient unto himself, and needs no outward ordinances for his guidance, save during his minority. The conservative, on the other hand, or the advocate of the present, affirms the inherent depravity of man, affirms that he is insufficient unto himself, and requires the dominion of tutors and governors all his appointed days upon the earth. This accordingly is the quarrel which has first to be settled—the quarrel between Socialism and Civilization, before men will care in any considerable numbers to balance the claims of rival socialists. Let it first of all be made plain to us that Socialism is true in idea, is true as against Civilization ; then we shall willingly enough discuss the relative superiority of St. Simon to Owen, or of Fourier to both.

How then shall this grand preliminary quarrel be settled ? Of course, historically or actually, it will be settled only by the march of events. But how shall it be settled meanwhile, intellectually, or to your and my individual satisfaction? Each of us, doubtless, will judge it in the light of his own ideas and aspirations. If, for example, Socialism appear to promise better things than Civilization to the highest life of man, we cannot fail, of course, to bid it God-speed, and predict its speedy triumph. If the reverse judgment should ensue, we shall, equally of course, execrate it, and leave it to the contempt of mankind. Now it is of no consequence to my hearer to be apprized of my private attitude with respect to this controversy. Yet his own decision may be helped one way or the other, either for Socialism or against it, by a fair scrutiny of the grounds on which any intelligent person has already come to a conclusion. Accordingly, I will not hesitate frankly to declare the method of my own understanding in dealing with this controversy.

Our design being then to try Socialism and Civilization by the bearing they respectively exert upon the destiny of man, or his highest life, let me first of all declare my conception of that destiny.

Man's destiny is, to become sufficient unto himself, or what is the same thing, to become both the object and subject of his own action. This is his destiny or perfect life, because it exactly images the divine life. We call God perfect or infinite, because He is sufficient unto Himself. And we call Him sufficient unto Himself, because His power is unlimited by any thing external to Him, or what is the same thing, because the object of His action falls in every case within His own subjectivity. The perfection of action consists in the internality of the object to the subject. Every action is genuine or perfect which expresses this internality, which expresses the inward taste or personality of the subject. And every action is spurious or imperfect which expresses the externality of the object to the subject, which exhibits the subject obeying some outward motive, either of natural desire or social obligation. Now inasmuch as God creates or gives being to all things, inasmuch as the universe has its total being in Him, his action knows no external object or end. As nothing exists out of Him, He cannot act from any outward motive or impulsion, but only from an inward joy or delight; and to act purely from an inward joy or delight, is to be sufficient unto one's self, and consequently infinite or perfect.

Such being the perfection of the Creator, it follows that the destiny of the creature, or his highest, his perfect, his infinite life, lies in his becoming the conscious source of his own action, in his becoming not merely the subject, but also the exclusive object of his own activity, in his becoming, in other words, like God, sufficient unto himself. You perceive that the very fact of his creatureship necessitates this destiny. To be a creature of God, is simply and in its largest statement, to reflect or image God, and man cannot reflect or image God, that is to say, cannot become a true creature of God, save in so far as he becomes the actual unity of internal and external, or of object and subject. God is the absolute unity of object and subject, or internal and external, because He alone has being, and therefore excludes all limitation, or definition. To become God's image therefore, man must become the actual unity of internal and external, or object and subject. He must be himself the unity of these two elements, must be himself the sole object, as well as the sole subject of all his activity. Thus the intensest individuality, an individuality amounting in every case to what we now call genius, is the birthright of man. He dishonors, he disavows his divine source until this birthright be universally vindicated. The vindication of it is in fact the very staple of human history, the very stuff out of which the whole vast fabric has been woven. For man has been vicious, that is, has warred with nature, only because nature unjustly claims his allegiance. And he has been criminal, that is, has warred with society, only because society holds him in unrighteous subjection.

The divinely-imposed destiny of man then, *the destiny imposed by the very fact of his creatureship*, involves his complete dominion both of nature and society. If man be the creature of God, then as God is infinite or perfect, or what is the same thing, as His power is unlimited by any thing external to Him, is unlimited by any thing but His own sovereign pleasure, so consequently man, His creature, is bound to exhibit the same infinitude or perfection, and achieve an equally universal dominion. He is pledged by the fact of his creatureship to exert a power unlimited by any thing external to him, by any thing but his own sovereign pleasure, and consequently, he is pledged to achieve the perfect empire both of nature and society. You cannot reflect for a moment on this fact of his creatureship, on the fact that God is the ALL of his life, without acknowledging that the power of man is at bottom the power of God ; without acknowledging in fact, that the substantial force or selfhood in every man is God. Hence you conclude that man is bound by an irrepressible divine instinct, that he is in truth divinely impelled to aspire after a complete conquest both of nature and society. They must both confess his lordship, must both render him perfect homage and furtherance, or suffer the chastisement of disobedience. Accordingly, so long as the subjugation of the physical and moral universe to the individual life is actually incomplete, and man's dignity as man consequently in abeyance, you find him asserting his rightful supremacy to both, if not in a normal and permanent way, why then by the ephemeral and loathsome methods of vice and crime. For vice is nothing else than man's instinctive revulsion against the dominion of his own body : rather than endure that dominion he destroys the body. And crime is nothing more than his instinctive revulsion against the dominion of society : rather than endure that dominion, he renounces, he destroys society. Philosophically regarded, vice and crime are simply negative assertions of man's sovereign individuality, of his divinely communicated and indefeasible responsibility to himself alone. They are the despised and disregarded prophets—prophets drunk with the wisdom of God, and therefore themselves, like all prophets, unenriched by it—of the ultimate dignity of the individual life, a dignity which shall be established upon the unlimited submission, and nurtured by the exhaustless bounty, both of nature and society.

But you will say, how is this possible? How shall the individual life become thus eminent over nature and society, without greater qualification than it now possesses ? Look at Lord —— on the other side of the water ; look at Bishop —— on this side. Both of these men have come into exalted place, into positions of wealth and social eminence, and you instantly perceive each to be an enthroned vanity, an enthroned flatulence, worthless because sycophantic to the governing class; worse than worthless to the subject class, because supported by them. What shall hinder you and me and every one from the conspicuous imbecility of these men ?

The inquirer errs by confounding things different. He confounds our natural and finite individuality with our spiritual or infinite one, which is a great oversight. The temporal and spiritual lordships he adduces are types or shadows—not substantial things, and now that the day has come for the substantial things themselves to claim inauguration in men's respect, the old worn-out types avouch their intrinsic stupidity by disputing ground with them. As well might the finger-post claim to be the city toward which it points, as these puny emblems claim to be the divine realities they barely indicate. I, on the contrary, am speaking altogether of the Divine Man, the legitimate Lord of heaven and earth, the man whom both Church and State, both priest and king, merely typify, and the shock of whose oncoming feet consequently now rocks every throne and altar in Christendom to their base, causing, in fact, the whole christian orb to reel to and fro like a drunken man. Let us consider the constitution of this man. Let us, in other words, consider the precise nature of our true or God-given individuality.

Our true individuality is our faculty of action, our power to do. By so much as I am able to do or produce, am I myself. A man *is* that which he *does*, neither more nor less. What I do, that I am. I possess both passion and intelligence, but neither of these things characterize *me;* they characterize all men, characterize my nature. What characterizes me, what gives me individuality, or distinctive genius, is my action. Thus all character is grounded in action ; all being grounded in doing ; all cause grounded in effect. This constitutes, according to Swedenborg, the glory of Deity, that He has no love nor wisdom apart from His power, neither *esse* nor *existere* apart from *procedere*. In other words, God's passion and intelligence, so to speak, subsist only in His action. In a briefer word still, God is essentially active.

But now observe : although action furnishes the

sole ground and measure of being, although, in
other words, man's true selfhood consists in his
faculty of action, yet we must carefully discriminate
the kind of action which constitutes that true or
divine selfhood. Our highest mode of action is æsthetic. Our proper individuality consequently, our
inmost and God-given genius, respires exclusively
the atmosphere of Art, and the Artist accordingly
stands forth as the sole and plenary Divine Man.
All action properly so called, all action which really
individualizes us, is essentially æsthetic. Not our
physical and moral action, or what we do from the
constraint of necessity and duty, but only our æsthetic action, or what we do from taste, from spontaneity, expresses our true or inmost personality.
Both our physical and moral action is obligatory,
denying us that freedom we have in God. They
are both enforced by penalties, and clearly a man
needs no penalties to enforce his doing what he
does of himself, or spontaneously. Whatever action is enforced by the alternative of suffering, confesses itself by that fact to be inappropriate to the
subject, to be a sheer imposition either of his physical or social relations. The action which is appropriate to him, which expresses his proper or
God-given genius, he does of himself, does sponta-

neously and without the urgency of any external
motive.

Accordingly both our physical and moral activity
fall under this condemnation. They neither of
them express, are neither of them appropriate to,
our divine or perfect individuality. They both express our infirm or finite individuality, that which
we derive from our relations to our own body and
our fellow man. I must obey my natural necessities and my social obligations, or suffer in the one
case physical, in the other moral, death. Hence I
am *quoad* my natural and social selfhood in incessant bondage to the fear of death. And you know
that our true or inmost individuality, that which we
derive from God, is incapable of death, is immortal.
It is the doom of the natural and moral man to
perish ; the internal or divine man survives their decay. Their decay constitutes for him in fact an in-
cident of progress, a condition of greater enfranchisement.

I say that death is the doom of the natural and
moral man. What I mean by this is, that neither
the natural nor the moral law is the law of life. Let
me seriously attempt to fulfil either of these laws, and
I sink into instant death. It is the peculiarity of
either law to deride all direct obedience, and accept

fulfilment at the hands of those only who are perfectly indifferent to it. Neither of them was intended to confer life upon man, but merely to celebrate and adorn a life flowing from an infinite source. Thus let me set myself perfectly to fulfil the law of nature, say, for example, to achieve perfect health of body, and I not only on the instant become the abject slave of my body, but kind nature herself, as if to scourge me out of such slavery, lets loose her whole artillery of destruction to lay me low in the dust—her winter's cold, her summer's heat, her myriad lurking miasms and pestilences. The only man whom nature respects, though she has at present a very imperfect respect for any man, the only man whom she feeds with her choicest juices and aromas, is the man who cares not a jot about her, and snaps his fingers equally at her curse and blessing. So also let me devote myself, with a view to life, to the fulfilling of the moral law, or the complete discharge of my obligations to my fellow-man, and instead of the life I covet, ten thousand deaths instantly open their mouths to sting me into despair and madness. The letter of the law appears brief and easy, but the moment I indulge the fatal anxiety, have I fulfilled it? I begin to apprehend its infinite spirit, the spirit of benevolence or charity, which prompts such an utter crucifixion of selfishness—such an incessant and immaculate deference to the will and even the whimsy of another, that I am worried and fretted into my grave, before I have really entered on my obedience—and the law which I fondly deemed to intend me life, turns out a minister of utter death.

The truth is, society like nature secretly despises the slave and reverences the freeman—despises the man who lives upon her favor, and worships him who tramples that favor under foot. Since the world has stood, no man of genius, no man of genuine inward force has ever announced himself, without society, in the long run, forgiving and justifying his most flagrant contempt of her authority. The grandest genius yet revealed on earth, a man with whose awful freedom the timid and servile genius of other men compares, as the bounded current of a river compares with the measureless expanse of ocean, defied to the last extremity the most sensitive, the most exacting and the most conceited society the world has ever known, and with what result? He never succumbed to it for one moment, from his cradle to his grave, never did and never said a thing that did not provoke its unmeasured hate, yet what has been the consequence? No one like him was ever found to have uttered the universal heart of man; he has been deified by the instinct of the most enlightened ages; churches, kingdoms, empires, worlds have baptized themselves in his name; pompous rituals hourly declare his praise; every one who stood in the most transient relation to him has been canonized; even the mother he disclaimed and the disciple he rebuked have been exalted into the matronage and patronage of heaven; the very instrument of his death has become symbolical of everlasting life; and all this, while as yet men have only known the meagerest and most fallacious surface of his sweetness, or while the actual truth of the case has appealed only to the blindness of instinct in them, utterly denying the confirmation of reason.

But the proposition needs no argument. A reference to our daily practical experience proves that we never confound a man's true individuality with his physical and social conditions. We never ascribe genius, character, divinity, to a man on the strength of his physical or moral excellence. We deem him indebted for the former to the bounty of nature, for the latter to the grace of God. We do not conceive of either as reflecting the slightest credit upon the man himself, as in the slightest de-

gree *appropriate* to himself. They are appropriate
to man universally, and in this point of view we do
them honor. We feel that no one has any special
title to these things, and that their possession therefore is a matter of pure accident. No one suspects
Cleopatra of possessing any private property in her
beauty, nor Dr. Channing any private property in
his virtue. Should such a suspicion get authenti-
cated, we should instantly declare these persons
enemies rather than ornaments of our common life,
because they took away or sequestered so much of
what should be a common possession. A beautiful
physique and a beautiful *morale* are both alike a gift
and not an achievement. They flow from a fortunate natural or a fortunate spiritual parentage, and
are utterly irrelevant to the true or divine individuality of the subject. Genius, which is the divine presence in man, visits alike the beautiful and those
who are destitute of beauty, and it consecrates the
annals of virtue not a whit more profusely than it
does those of crime.

No, we gladly recognise and honor both beauty
and virtue, but we forbid the subject to claim the
least property in either. On the contrary, when the
handsome man begins to esteem himself for his
beauty, and the upright man to prize his virtue, the

company of plain people and sinners becomes instantly sweet and refreshing. The truth is, every man in the exact ratio of his manhood is ashamed both of his beauty and his virtue, feeling himself to be so wholly unimplicated in either, feeling himself really in debt to a partial nature for the one, and a happy spiritual chance for the other. And no true man loves to be a debtor, loves in fact to be either debtor or creditor. Can any thing be so disastrous to all manhood as foppery, or pride in one's physical individuality? Yes, Pharisaism, or spiritual foppery, which signifies a pride in one's moral individuality. This is even more disastrous. But if the physical and moral life—the life of nature and the life of society, were the true divine life in man, then it were right for us to magnify our physical and moral attributes and make them public.

Wherefore I repeat that it is an infallible instinct of the strong man to conceal his strength, and of the virtuous man to renounce his virtue. Nature bids the one take no pride in his strength, the other to take no pride in his uprightness, under penalty of proving a nuisance. They are valuable possessions of man, but they constitute no true manhood. They are ornaments to be worn upon occasion, but should never be paraded. The jewels of a beautiful woman do not pretend to impart beauty, but only to signalize or celebrate it. When worn for their own sake, or worn by other than beautiful persons, they are designed merely as a tacit apology for the absence of beauty, as a sort of death's head or hatchment to indicate where beauty ought to be, but alas is not. For nature owes a form of immaculate grace and vigor to her sovereign lord, and the personal ornaments, which we his present deputies and representatives wear, may be viewed accordingly as so many evidences of nature's obligation, and so many pledges of its ultimate discharge. In the same manner, all relatively great physical and moral superiority should be regarded by the subject as insignia of an infirm and beggarly individuality, and should always be exerted under an inward protest. For why should man, the heir of infinitude, envy the horse his strength, the angel his goodness? Leave the horse his distinction, leave the angel his. God will not always leave His child mendicant upon the heavens above and the earth beneath, but will fast reduce both of these into the joyful service of his great supremacy.

Behold then the fact : all our individually-characteristic action is æsthetic, or expresses our inward taste. I have no property in any action, no

action truly represents and belongs to me, unless the
object of it be within me, unless it reflect my private or distinctive genius, unless, in short, it be
creative and embody some idea. Hence we have
an infallible test of our true or God-given individuality. For individuality, character, being, proprium, self hood, personality, whatever you please
to call the inmost vital fact in man, stands in action.
Thus our true individuality is neither physical nor
moral. It is purely æsthetic. It stands in our relation neither to nature nor to our fellow-man, but
exclusively to God, who is our inmost life. He
alone is truly self-pronounced—he alone divinely
vivified—who acts neither from physical nor social
control—neither from necessity nor duty—but purely from delight or attraction, and this emphatically
is the Artist. He alone acts from inspiration, or from
within outwards. The natural man obeys the law
of his finite body. The moral man obeys the law
of his finite fellow, the law of society. But the Artist—and when I use the word Artist, I do not mean
any special functionary, as the poet, painter, or musician; I mean the man of whatsoever function,
from king to cobbler, who follows his function from
taste and not from necessity nor duty, who culti-
vates it not with a view merely to a livelihood or to

fame, but purely because he loves it and finds it its
own exceeding great reward—but the Artist, or Divine Man obeys the infinite law of God as manifested in the inspirations of his own soul. He alone accordingly attracts the unbribed homage of mankind.
All men of every religion and complexion unite to
do him honor. He breaks down every middle wall
of partition which ignorance and superstition have
erected between Jew and Gentile, saint and sinner,
and makes of the twain one new man. Hence the
Artist claims to be the reconciling or uniting term
between God and man, the spiritual or infinite reality symbolized by the literal or finite God-man,
the wholly incontestible son of God, the heir of all
divine power majesty and glory, by whom alone
God estimates the world.

But if this be so, then it will be perceived that
the question put to me may be very easily answer-
ed.   That is to say, it will be seen that the eminence which I claim for the individual, is not that
mere usurped or conventional eminence exhibited
by Lord This and Bishop That, and based upon
their subservience to sundry political and ecclesiastical interests, but an eminence which springs out of
the real divine worth of every individual, out of
God's most vital presence and force within him, and

which is cordially ratified therefore by nature and society. For the Artist, the man of genius, the man of ideas, is not elected supreme; he is born so. He is not obliged to canvass for votes. He only needs to reveal himself to command all votes, because he is utterly without a competitor. For the Artist is not good by comparison merely, or the antagonism of meaner men. He is positively good, good by absolute or original worth, good like God, good in himself, and therefore universally good. He daily enriches nature and society with new acquisitions of beauty. For the bread and the wine— for the material and spiritual nourishment they afford him, he returns to their own bosoms good measure, heaped up, pressed down, and running over, for he mediates between them and God, bringing down and making visible to them the infinite splendor of Deity, while, at the same time, developing their own answering fecundity, harmony, beauty and joy.

Such being our conception of human destiny, of man's perfect life, I think you will decide that Socialism exhibits a far more benignant aspect towards it than civilization does. For the great obstacle at present to the divine life in man is the domination of society, is the preponderance of the

moral or social element over the æsthetic or individual one in human affairs. The sentiment of responsibility grinds human life into the dust. It
crushes the divine aroma or spirit out of it, thus de-
stroying the whole grace of the fashion of it. It is
very important that I be under innocent relations to
my own body and to my fellow-man ; it is very important that these relations be full of peace and
amity ; but it is of an altogether infinite importance to me that I experience right relations to God
or my inmost life. Indeed the former relations derive all their worth from the latter. If it were not
that I am inwardly one with God, that I am destined
to the inheritance of His infinitude or perfection, and
consequently to a life of universal benignity, it
would be of no moment what relations I sustained
either to nature or my fellow-man. It would be of
no moment beyond the immediate satisfaction of my
appetites, whether the relation were one of concord
or discord. But since on the one hand I am destined, by the very fact of my creatureship, to an actual fellowship of the divine perfection, and since,
on the other hand, all perfection implies the actual
unity of object and subject—of substance and form
—of internal and external—so consequently it is of
vital interest to me, that my external relations,

which are my relations to nature and man, accurately reflect my internal ones, which are my relations to God, and present a precisely commensurate unity with them. But if this be so, if the worth of my outward ties flow down from the superior worth of my inward ones, then it is at once obvious to you that these latter ties are of primary importance, and should never be controlled by the former. If the main fact of my life be my unity with God, and the secondary or derivative fact be my unity with nature and man, then clearly this subordinate interest should not dominate or exclude the essential one. This is plain. But now how stands the fact?

I have no hesitation in affirming, that the fact is exactly counter to the truth. I have no hesitation in affirming, that society, as at present, or rather as heretofore, constituted, arrays the lower interest in conflict with the higher, and debases man into abject slavery to itself. Society affords no succor to the divine life in man. Any culture we can give to that life, is owing not to society, but to our fortunate independence of it. For the incessant action of society is to shut up all my time and thought to the interests of my mere visible existence, to the necessity of providing subsistence, education, and social respect for myself and my

4*

children. To these narrow limits society confines
all my passion, all my intellect, all my activity ;
and so far denies me self-development. My true
or divine selfhood is completely swamped in transient frivolous cares. Indeed so rigorous is our social tyranny, so complete a servitude does society
impose upon the individual, that we have almost
lost the tradition of our essential freedom, and
scarcely one in a million believes that he has any
individuality or sacredness apart from his natural
and social ties. He who constitutes our private and
distinctive individuality, He who ceaselessly pants
to become avouched and appropriated to every man
as his nearest and most inseparable self, is for the
most part banished from the glowing heart of humanity, into frigid and extramundane isolation,
so that we actually seem to have no life above the
natural and social spheres.

But this appearance is fallacious. It is a correspondence of that fallacy of the senses which makes
the earth central, and the heavens circumferential.
I will not deny that the most genial relations bind
God and my body, bind God and my neighbor ;
but I will deny *totis viribus* that either my body or
my neighbor forms the true point of contact between God and me. He is infinitely nearer to

me than my own body; infinitely nearer to me also than my neighbor. In short He is with me not only finitely but infinitely, not only by the medium of the physical and moral life, but also in my spontaneous attractions and tendencies. Here preeminently do I find God. Here alone do I behold the infinite Beauty. Here alone do I perfectly lose myself and perfectly find myself. Here alone, in short, do I feel empowered to say, what every true creature of God is bound to say : I and my father are one.

I repeat that the whole strain of society is adverse to this spontaneous and divine life in man. It relegates his whole energy to the service of his physical and moral interest, that is to its own direct advantage, and beyond this point takes no cognizance of him. It utterly ignores his proper, God-given, and æsthetic life, the life whose supreme law is the good pleasure of the subject ; or recognises it only to profane and corrupt it. It is melancholy to see the crawling thing which society christens Art, and feeds into fawning sycophancy. It has no other conception of Art than as polished labor, labor stripped of its jacket and apron, and put into parlor costume. The Artist is merely the aboriginal ditcher refined into the painter, poet, or sculptor.

Art is not the gush of God's life into every form of spontaneous speech and act ; it is the talent of successfully imitating nature—the trick of a good eye, a good ear, or a good hand. It is not a really infinite life, consubstantiate with the subject and lifting him into ever new and unpremeditated powers and achievements ; it is an accomplishment, a grace to be learned, and to be put off and on at one's convenience.

Accordingly society establishes academies of Art, gives out rules for its prosecution, and issues diplomas to the Artist, by which he may be visibly discriminated from ordinary people. But always on this condition, that he hallow, by every work of his hands, its existing prejudices and traditions ; that he devote his perfectly docile genius to the consecration of its morality. If he would be truly its child, let him confine himself to the safe paths of portraiture and bust making, to the reproduction of the reigning sanctities in church and state, their exemplary consorts and interesting families. By this door many of our aspiring " artists " have entered the best society. But if the disciple be skittish, and insist on " sowing the wild oats " of his genius, let him, at most, boldly allegorize the Calvinistic divinity or the Unitarian morality into Voyages of Life

and similar contrivances, or dash off ineffectual bri-
gands and Magdalens that should find no forgiveness
in this world or the next. But these things are tri-
vial. If society did no greater harm to God's life
in man than to misconceive the nature and misapply
the name of Art, it would be foolish to complain.
But the evil it does is positive and profound, and
justifies a perfectly remorseless criticism.

For the true complaint against society is not the
little it does actually to promote the divine life in
man, but the much it does actually to hinder that
life by giving him a conscience of sin against God,
and so falsifying the true relation between them. If
I fail in my allegiance to society, if I violate any of
its enactments, in forcibly taking, for example,
the property of my neighbor, society is not thereupon content to visit me with the penalty provided
for the case : it has the hardihood also to proclaim
me a sinner against God, and threaten me with His
wrath. Society has the presumption to identify its
own will with the will of God. It assumes that
whatsoever it declares to be property, or to belong
to A., B. and C., is also viewed as such property,
or as so belonging, on the part of God ; and that
hence in violating this property I offend God no
less than itself. Certainly it is contrary to the di-

vine will that any man should violate his neigh-
bour's property.   We may say that such a thing is
absolutely contrary to the divine will, and cannot
therefore be done.   It would be an aspersion of the
divine power to say that He gave me a property
which any other man had power to take away from
me.   Or it would be an aspersion of His goodness
to suppose Him giving me a certain property, and
at the same time giving another power to deprive
me of it.   The whole conception of a man really
sinning against God is intolerably puerile.

The error of society herein lies in its giving man
what Swedenborg calls a *false proprium*, that is a
property which God does not give him.   Society
does all it can to finite man, to include or shut up
his proprium, his selfhood, within itself, and so
render him its abject vassal or dependent.   The
more external property it gives him, the more
houses, lands, flocks, and perishable goods of all
sorts, the more it finites him and renders him dependent on itself.   For society alone confers and
guarantees this property.   Abstract the protection
of society, and no man could keep it a day.   God,
on the contrary, seeks incessantly to aggrandize His
child, and render him *in-finite*.   He strives to insin-
uate a proprium, which shall lift him above all out-

ward limitation. He makes Himself over to him in an inward and invisible way, and so endows him with a property both incorruptible and inviolable, which no moth can corrupt, and no thief break through and steal.

Undoubtedly every man's enjoyment of God involves his enjoyment also of nature and his fellow-man. Undoubtedly every man possesses a natural and social proprium or selfhood as well as a divine one; for the latter exacts the former as its own basis. What I complain of is that the former should be forever kept so disproportionate to the latter. I complain that I who am as to my inward parts infinite or perfect, should find no answering perfection in my circumstances. I who am inwardly one with God—ONE I say, not *identical*, for identity destroys unity—should be one also with nature and my fellow-man. My natural and social proprium should be precisely commensurate with my inward or divine one. Whatsoever the whole of nature has to bestow, whatever blessing the unlimited fellowship of mankind encloses, should be mine by virtue of my inward worth. Nature and society should have no power to identify me with a particular potato-patch and a particular family of mankind all my days. The fact of my divine genesis makes God's

whole earth my home, makes all His children my
intimates and brethren. Why should nature have
power to limit this home, society have power to limit
this brotherhood ? Their true function is only to
universalize me, and give me outward development
commensurate with my inward power. They but
cheat me when they give me houses and lands, and
a score of friends, and call these things my property. They are not my property. My true property in nature includes all her strengths and sweet-
nesses, includes all her resources to make pliant and
strong and beautiful my body, and give my spirits
the play of the morning breeze. And my true property in mankind is not my mere natural father and
mother and brother and sister, and the great tiresome dispensation of uncles and aunts and cousins
and nieces thereunto appended, but the whole vast
sweep of God's harmonies in the realms of human
passion, intellect, and action. Nature is my debtor
and foe until she have deposited all her pith within
me, and given me a body superior to her thunders.
Society is likewise my debtor and foe until she
have given me the frankest fellowship of every man,
until she have lavished upon me the really inex-
haustible wealth of human affection, and sunned

me with the really infinite splendors of human thought.

In one word let nature give *herself* to man, and society give *herself*, as is but fitting where God does not hesitate to give Himself. Shall these have the assurance to offer but a part, where he gives all? God gives His infinite self to me. And this property is inalienable in all ways. Not only it cannot be stolen; it cannot even be lent. The fine genius or faculty of Shakspeare could not be transferred by him to his friend. He could give his friend all he possessed, all his affection, all his thought, all his bodily service. But he could not give him his genius, his selfhood, his faculty of action. This was not his possession. It possessed him rather, and it was possessed only of God. It was, in fact, God in him.

Besides, suppose me to possess a large conventional property in land or money. Suppose me hereupon to address this, that, and the other needy friend, saying, " Let no law divide us ; let us share and share alike, cut and come again," and so forth. Do you not instantly feel that it would be more noble and human for me to do this, than to make these needy friends thieves in heart, by summoning the law to give them perpetual exclusion ? In this case do I not rise superior to the law ? Do you not perceive therefore that the law was made only for man, not man for the law ? Do you not feel, in short, that all law was given only as a foil or set-off to our magnanimity, only that we might, *by virtue of our plenary manhood*, utterly renounce and abrogate it ?

How sheer an idleness then to tell me that I have robbed a man of property divinely given ! Any property which it was in my power to take from him was not peculiarly proper to him. It was at least quite as proper to me, or I could not have coveted it. When God gives me a coat, no rogue in Christendom shall be cunning enough to coax it off my shoulders. And when He sends us wives, the statute against adultery will confess itself superfluous.

Society, however, is at present founded upon this atrocious calumny towards God and man, that they are essentially inimical to each other ; and both God and man consequently are working its speedy downfall. Interposing between man and his inmost life, it represents that life to be death, and drives him consequently to madness. Professing to be the husbandman of God's vineyard, when He looks to it for grapes, it brings

Him forth only wild grapes. When He makes an inquisition for man, His image, society mocks Him with a hideous rabble of murderers, thieves, harlots and liars. It obscures, it defiles God's righteousness in every soul of man. Will He long endure such a husbandman ? Does He not prize the vineyard above the husbandman, and will He not soon utterly destroy the latter from the face of the earth ?

Society pronounces me an evil man, by virtue of my having violated sundry of her statutes. But what shall statutes say for themselves that are capable of violation ? Shall they pretend to be divine? This were blasphemous. For who ever heard of God's statutes being violated, of God's will being frustrated ? The imagination is childish. The divine power is perfect, which means that it never encounters opposition. Yet I have heard theologians aver that God has given man power to obey or disobey His statutes at pleasure. Wherefore then should they represent God as complaining ? If He have given man power to obey or disobey, as he pleases, then the exercise of this power in either direction, must be grateful to Him. If He leave me free to obey or disobey Him, you defame Him when you make

Him resent my exercise of this freedom. If you give your child permission to go to Cambridge or Roxbury as he pleases, and then denounce him to the constables for going to the latter place, you make yourself unworthy of the child, proving yourself not a parent but a tyrant. The child would despise you if he were not your child, and the legitimate heir therefore of your meanness—if you had not first defrauded him of his fair spiritual proportions by begetting him. No! since the world has stood, the law of God has known no violation. And no better evidence can be had that a law is undivine, and therefore only capable of violation, than the fact of its having actually been violated.

I admit then, that I am, according to the decree of society, an evil man. As measured by its appointments, by its institutions, I am an unmitigated liar, murderer, thief, and adulterer. But now I appeal to a higher judicatory, and summon society itself as a criminal before the bar of God. Here stand I, a creature of God, a thing God-made from the crown of my head to the soul of my foot. There stand certain ordinances of society, certain appointments made by man, which I have violated. The violation is undeniable. It has not been once only but a myriad times. It has been, if you please, both thorough and remorseless. In God's sight then where does the fault attach? To the God-made thing, or the man-made?

If we say "to the former," will not God frown us dumb? Does He see any evil in the work of His own hands? The supposition were instantly fatal to the universe of creation, for it saps the creative perfection. No, God decides by the absolute constraint of His perfection, that the true criminal in this case is society, that if I, His child, have broken any law, it was only because that law was itself or primarily a violation of my essential liberty, the liberty I have in Him. How should I, His creature, and therefore as pure in my inward parts as He himself, become a thief, unless society tempted me by giving some one else an exclusive property in that which every want of my nature makes equally appropriate to me? How should I become an adulterer unless society affirmed some one else to possess an exclusive property in some person, whom the very fact of the adultery proves to belong equally to me? How should I become a false-witness and murderer, unless society, by putting me at a disadvantage with other men, by ensuring them a superior social position, and a more

affluent supply of nature's wants, steadfastly com-
mended them to my envy and enmity?

It is solely because society itself violates the
unity of creation by the institution of false and in-
jurious *propria* among men, that I become a criminal. The divine spirit within me prompts a perfect love to all mankind—prompts me to abound in
every office of respect and affection. How shall
this spirit get actual organization, so long as society
arrays me against every one else, and every one
else against me, so long as it makes my interest
clash with the interest of every man in the community? Let society allow my native and God-
given appetency to be the sole measure of my outward enjoyment, then my relations with nature and
society will become instantly harmonious.

Such is the wrong society does its children. It
first makes them scoundrels, and then sets God to
hunt them down. It was not always thus. There
was a time when the Christian Church had life and
walked the earth as the friend of man. Society then
had no power to sap the hope of the humblest
wretch. Let him have actually festered with
crime, let him have violated every statute of society, and proved himself a perpetual terror to his
species, yet society found no craven priest to deny him

mercy with God.   The church confronted its utmost
venom, and said to the loathsome victim, " confide
in me and you shall be safe—receive my anointing
and you shall stand absolved from all guilt."   The
church was then a power only and not an intelligence. It had no rationality.   It disclaimed all
philosophy.   It knew not and cared not to justify
its great pretension. It knew only the name of God,
and believed only in his unquestionable sovereignty.
Its reverence was only the blindest of instincts, yet
that instinct gave it power to shelter and sanctify
every form of human passion however actually
perverted.

Accordingly, it is inexpressibly touching to see
with what infinite assurance the baited and hunted
criminal, every pore running blood, and his tongue
lapping out, as he fled from the vengeance of his
pursuers, always betook himself to the altar of God,
to find peace and refreshment.   We may laugh at
this, we who pay our clergy as we do our cooks, to
do us a prescribed service, that is, to convert the
popular hope of heaven and fear of hell into guarantees of our social tranquillity.   But the service done
to humanity by the old clergy is wholly inestimable
in money.   The diamonds of Golconda and the
gold of California are of no worth beside it, for in

the nascent mind of society, they implanted and inwove the inextinguishable dread of a power superior to itself, a power which gives to the humblest individual a sacredness above the stability of its proudest throne.

Nothing but this function, the function of antagonizing society and forbidding it to dominate the individual life, justifies the existence of the church. If God's primary thought were for society, and not for man, if the main aim of His providence were to render man morally good, that is to make him willingly subject to his fellow-man, then the church directly contravened this intention, and exposed itself to the charge of profligacy. But if society were God's secondary care and man the primary, if God designed to endow man with self-sovereignty and make him a law unto himself, if He would give the personal or æsthetic element supremacy, and make the moral and physical elements completely subordinate, then the church, with all her blindness and irrationality, stands forth as God's righteous servant. For it was this interest which the church unflinchingly though unconsciously espoused; it was this interest which it fostered and developed in spite of the poverty of nature and the dogmatism of society. **Man's** true individuality, the sovereign or divine humanity, was yet unfulfilled on earth. He who had alone asserted and revealed it under negative conditions had gone away, leaving the church to carry out his quarrel. Thus the church stood for and represented the sovereignty of the individual life over nature and society. To this old ecclesiasticism accordingly are we primarily indebted for all that opulence of private worth which is now fast tarnishing the lustre of governments and teaching man to reverence himself above the longest-descended institutions.

It is, of course, silly enough to look upon the old church as possessing any positive worth, to look upon those filthy old popes and fat-headed priests as possessing any real divine recognition. But view them as representing the divine humanity still latent in time, as symbolizing the sovereign lord of nature and society yet to come, and their sanctity becomes instantly radiant and credible. What seems a most impudent pretension when urged in its own behalf, becomes the most natural thing in the world in behalf of its client.

The old hierarchy suffers, because our eyes have become disenchanted by gazing on the modern one. The modern church claims to be something in itself—claims to possess no longer a symbolical but

5

a positive sanctity—to be an actual divine product on the earth. But in order to justify this pretension and find favor with mankind, it is obliged of course to sell itself to the state, that is, to espouse the current life of society. For if the church obtruded a really superior life upon society, to that which society itself generates, conflict would ensue, and the church would be incontinently strangled. Thus the church, now-a-days, in order to escape being murdered, commits suicide. Accordingly you now find no conflict between church and state. The church ducks her obeisant head, and takes whatever position the state allows her, giving in return her countenance and practical advocacy to every institution, corrupt or incorrupt, which society approves.

In this state of things you necessarily miss the church's old renown. When she merges her ideal in the actual, she stultifies herself, becomes extinct, since her whole office was to foretell and prepare the way of a perfect actual. What is the use of a church to enforce the life of the state? What sort of a deity is he who sanctions the current morality of any political society under heaven, political or religious society either? No man believes in such a deity *ex animo*, but only by tradition, by zealous tuition. Consequently no man believes in such a church.

Thus the church gave up all her power over the human heart when she became the stipendiary and tool of the state, when she ceased to storm in upon society tidings of God's irreversible scorn. This was an office worthy of her, to hold God so unmix-ed with all human quarrels, so untouched by all human distinctions, as to be alike favorable to the judge on the bench and the felon on the gibbet. What a descent from this to our present church—a church which has no ideal beyond the State, and instead of claiming, most conscientiously *renounces* the power of immortal life! Can such a church prefer any claim upon human affection save as a powerful police agency? Preposterous!

When one went to some old unscrupulous Hilde-brand and laid bare his deformities, he returned home healed of all disquiets, for he was sure of heaven, having received the palpable earnest of it into his stomach. When I go to any of our diluted clergy, to Bishop This, or Doctor That, or Reverend T'other, I find none of them bold enough to affirm my salvation. I may enter either of their churches and diligently pursue all its ordinances, but whether my destiny shall be upwards or downwards re-

mains a wholly inscrutable problem, to be cleared
up only by the event. Fie on such an imbecile
church ! It is a mere garnish for the corruptions of
society, a mere veil to soften iniquities which would
otherwise be intolerable.

But this is a digression. If the evils I have described be real, if civilization be fraught with these
and all other forms of hindrance to the divine life,
then clearly civilization stands condemned by its
fruits, and has no title to prejudice the promise of
Socialism. Socialism claims to be nothing more
than a remedy for the physical and moral ills which
inhere in civilization, which result from its very
genius. The whole promise of Socialism may be
thus summed up.—It promises to lift man out of
the harassing bondage which he is under to nature
and society, out of that crushing responsibility
which he is under to his own body and his fellow-
man, and so leave him subject forever to God's unimpeded inspiration, leave him, in fact, the very
play-thing of God, a mere pipe for the finger of
Deity to play what stops it pleases. It proceeds
upon a double postulate, namely, that every creature of God, by virtue of his creation, is entitled,
1, to an ample physical subsistence, that is, to the
satisfaction of all his natural appetites ; 2, to an

ample social subsistence, that is, to the respect and affection of every other creature of God. Whatever institution violates these principles by non-conformity, it pronounces tyrannous and void.

Thus Socialism condemns, after a certain stage of human progress, the institution of limited property. It demands for man an infinite property, that is to say a property in universal nature and in all the affections and thoughts of humanity. It is silly to charge it with a tendency to destroy property. It aims indeed to destroy all merely limited and conventional property, all such property as is held not by any inward fitness of the subject, but merely by external police or convention ; but it aims to destroy even this property only in the pacific way of superseding it, that is, by giving the subject possession of the whole earth, or a property commensurate with his inward and essential infinitude.

This, I confess, is what attracts me in the programme of Socialism, the unconscious service it renders to the divine life in me, the complete inauguration and fulfilment it affords to the Christian hope of individual perfection. Christianity is a virtual denial of all mystery to Deity, and an affirmation of His essential intelligibility. It denies to Deity any mere passive or inoperative perfection, and affirms His existence exclusively within human conditions. It reveals a perfect harmony between God in His infinitude and man in his lowest natural and social debasement, even when devoid of all physical grace and comeliness, and when despised, cast out, and rejected of the best virtue of his time. In short it affirms the unity of God and Man. Two things hinder the consciousness of this unity on the part of man—nature and society, the one by limiting his power, the other by limiting his sympathies ; the one by finiting his body, the other by finiting his soul. Accordingly, the Christ, or representative Divine Man, is seen warring with and subjugating both nature and society, making time and space so fluent and plastic to his desires as to avouch his actual bodily infinitude, and exerting so wholly genial an influence upon the opposite extremes of society—saint and sinner, Jew and Gentile,—as to avouch his equal spiritual infinitude.

Now what is here typically reported of the Christ is to be actually fulfilled in universal humanity, in every man, according to the promise, " What things ye see me do, ye shall do also, and greater things than these." Nature and society are to be glorified into the footstool of Almighty God, enshrined in every human bosom. I have no idea that man will ever be able literally to change water into wine, or to feed his body upon inadequate food, or to pass through stone walls at pleasure, or to satisfy the tax-gatherer out of the mouth of fishes. But I believe that the various internal reality of these symbols will be fully accomplished in us, that nature and society will become in the progress of science so vivid with divine meaning, that the infinite desire of man will receive a complete *present* satisfaction, and that instead of our relegating the vision of God, as now, to an exclusively *post-mortem* experience, He will become revealed to the natural senses with such an emphasis as to make the most frolicsome sports of childhood more worshipful than all piety.

Now Socialism alone supplies the science of this great consummation. It reveals the incessant operation of laws by which man's physical and social relations will be brought into the complete subjection of his inward or divine personality. It is the demonstration of a plenary unity between man and nature and man and man. It convinces me of infinitely more extended relations to nature than those which now define me, and of infinitely sweeter ties with man than those which bind me to the Tom,

Dick and Harry of my present chance acquaint-
anceship.

Let this unity then become visible, become organized, and I shall instantly realize the divine freedom, realize my true and infinite selfhood. For
then I shall become released from this finite and
false *proprium* which now enslaves me and keeps
me grovelling in the dust. If I am one with nature
and my fellow-man, if there be a sovereign unity
and not enmity pervading all our reciprocal relations, then clearly every appetite and affection both
of my physical and moral nature become instantly
legitimated, and I stand henceforth absolved from
all defilement, a new creature of God triumphant
over death and hell, nay more, taking death and
hell into friendly subjection, and suffusing their
hitherto dusk and dejected visages with the roseate
flush of omnipresent and omnipotent Life.

I repeat that the curse of our present ties, that
which eliminates all their poetry, is our limited property in men and things, is the finite selfhood imposed on us by the present evil world. My internal
property or selfhood, that which God gives me, is
nothing short of infinite, is Himself in truth. To
match this divine internal, nature gives me my
feeble body, society gives me a petty score of rela-

tives and friends. Whilst I accept this niggardly service from nature and society, whilst I strive to compel my internal aspirations within these outward bounds, I suffer torments which are appeased only to be renewed. This body is incompetent to the subjugation of nature which my spirit demands. I may battle stoutly for a while, but I accomplish after all only a grave. But suppose the battle to have been never so successful in a material point of view, suppose me to have realized any amount of superfluous potatoes, yet after all how mere a potato-cask do I remain, destitute of inward pith and riches! The battle with nature, the battle for animal subsistence, leaves us merely animal, leaves us actually unvivified of God, leaves us only the dimmest and most fluctuating hope of God in realms beyond the grave.

But society imposes the most torturing disability. Affiliating me to one man, and that man incapable seven times out of eight of supplying my bare necessities; restricting me to the fraternity of two or three persons whom probably the penury of our joint resources converts into mutual rivals and foes; committing my profoundest passional interests to the keeping of one frail will; turning the most sacred depths of passion within me into an arena of

5 *

public traffic, into material of habitual and vulgar gossip; society does its utmost to ensure me a daily profanation, and turn God's otherwise joyful force in me into the force of a giant despair, into the force of an eventual deadly retribution.

Let any one consider for a moment the best endowment he gets from present society, or the extent of limitation it imposes upon him, and then reply whether it can be long tolerable to God.

In the first place, we have the tie of the insulated family, which enjoins a superior affection to all involved in it than to any others. Let my father's interests clash with his neighbors; let my mother and the mother of any body else, come into rivalry; let my brother or sister conceive a quarrel with any unrelated person : you know that in all these cases I am a natural partisan, and that if I should practically disown the obligation, that blissful home which furnishes the theme of so much sincere as well as dishonest sentimentality, would become on the instant a very hell incapable of pacification. Conduct so unnatural on my part, no matter how just it might be in the abstract, would convert these natural brethren into my envenomed foes, and even disqualify me for any very cordial welcome from their original antagonist, the person for whose cause

I had forsaken theirs. Take the tie of township or country, that which generates the old-fashioned virtue called patriotism, and you see it to be full of the same iniquitious bondage.

In fact there exists no tie either natural or social, as society is now constituted, which does not tend to slavery, which does not cheat man's soul of its fair proportions. I love my father and mother, my brother and sister, but I deny their unconditional property in me. Society having been incompetent hitherto to fulfil its duties to me, has deputed the care and sustenance of my tender years to them. I acknowledge gratefully the kindness I have received at their hands. But if they ask any other reward for this kindness than the satisfaction of seeing me a man, if they expect me to continue their humble satellite and partisan, instead of God's conscript and votary solely, I am bound to disappoint them. I will be the property of no person, and I will accept property in no person. I will be the son of my father, and the husband of my wife, and the parent of my child, but I will be all these things in a thoroughly divine way, or only as they involve no obloquy to my inward righteousness, only as they impose no injustice on me toward others.

You all remember those grand mystic sayings of

the Christ, " whoso will lose his life in this world shall keep it unto life eternal," and " whoso will leave father or mother, or brother or sister, or wife or child, for my sake, shall find all these relations multiplied a hundred-fold." Now what is the great spiritual burden of these divine words, for you know every divine word is so mainly from within. Is it not that our primary dignity is divine, and flows from God within us instead of from our outward relations? Is it not that each of us is under paramount allegiance to his own spontaneous life, and that if we insist first on the fulfilment of this allegiance, all these secondary or derivative relations will fall of themselves into harmony ?

But you know this truth experimentally also. You know that you never find perfect peace or contentment in your outward and finite *proprium*. You know by experience that you cannot set your life's happiness upon any outward possession, be it wife or child, or riches, without an incessant and shuddering dread of betrayal. The infinite faculty within you steadfastly refuses these limited satisfactions. But when you rejoice first of all in that infinite faculty, when you seek above all things to give it development by the medium of appropriate action, by the medium of Art, then the house of your peace is built upon a rock, against which the windows of heaven are opened in vain. Let a man then renounce all enforced property in persons and things, accepting only such things and persons as actually gravitate to him ; let him renounce all tale-bearing and recourse to the police, and come into universal candor, into complete whiteness of soul towards all men and things, how instantly would every heart expand to him as to God's melting sunshine, and the earth swarm with fragrant kisses for his feet!

To become possible, however, in any great degree for the individual man, this quality of manhood must first become universal, and to make it universal is the function of Socialism, is the aim of social science. Socialism lifts us out of these frivolous and pottering responsibilities we are under to man, and leaves us under responsibility to God alone, or our inmost life. The way it does this, is by revealing the existence and operation of laws, which shall provide every man, woman, and child, the orderly and ample satisfaction of their natural appetites and affections, the unlimited expansion of their intellect, and the complete education of their faculty of action, however infinitely various that faculty may be. In short it reveals the method of man's perpetual re-creation, a re-creation so complete that every day shall come clad to him with all the freshness of God's dewy hand, stifling both memory and hope in the amplitude of a present bliss. Suppose Socialism then to have attained its end, suppose the Divine Life to have become by its means universalized, what a temple of enchantment this lacerated earth would become! For when all things and persons become free, become self-pronounced, then a universal reverence and truth spring up, every manifestation of character claiming and enjoying the homage we now pay only to unmanifested Deity.

Besides we degrade and disesteem whatsoever we absolutely own. We degrade by owning and just in the degree of our owning. It is a proverb, that no man values the good he has in hand, but only that which is to come. This is signally true in respect to persons. We degrade and disesteem every person we own absolutely, every person bound to us by any other tenure than his own spontaneous affection. Of course one values one's brothers and sisters in the present state of things, if from nothing else, then from self-love; for society is so unfriendly and torpid to us that the domestic hearth gathers a warmth not wholly its own. But who is ever found idealizing a brother or sister? Our instinct of Friendship is profaned where a brother is the claimant, and Love expires of sheer self-loathing in the presence of a sister.

It is the indispensable condition of a perfect respect, that a person be inwardly individualized, that is, possess the complete supremacy of his own actions. Then all his relations are of an inevitable dignity. When the wife of Quisquis declined his merely dutiful or voluntary allegiance, when she insisted upon erasing the marriage-bond as a stain upon his truth, and giving to their relation the sole sanction of spontaneity, her husband found that relation instantly glorified, or purged of its abundant meanness. His home became henceforth a livelier sanctuary than the church, and his wife a diviner page than all the prophets. So also one's child, how tiresome he grows when he does nothing morning, noon or night, but reflect the paternal dulness, when he is sedulous to do all the father prescribes and avoid all the mother condemns! Yet how beautiful he becomes, when he ever and anon flashes forth some spontaneous grace, some self-prompted courtesy!

Why is it esteemed disgraceful for the mature man to consult his natural father and mother in every enterprise, and be led by their advice ? The cause of this judgment is spiritual, and lies in the truth that man is destined by the fact of his divine genesis to self-sufficiency, to self-government, that he is destined to find all guidance within him and none whatever without him, and that he cannot persist accordingly in the infantile habit of seeking help beyond himself without flagrant detriment to his manhood, to his destiny. All our natural and social phenomena, in fact, are symbolic, and have no worth apart from the spiritual verities they embalm and typify.

To conclude, Socialism promises to make God's great life in man possible, promises to make all our relations so just, so beautiful and helpful, that we shall be no longer conscious of finiteness, of imperfection, but only of life and power utterly infinite. I am not able to satisfy any one's reasonable curiosity on this subject. Every one who trusts in a living and therefore active God, in that God who is quite as active and original in our day as He was six thousand years ago, in short every one whose hope for humanity is alert, behooves to acquaint himself forthwith with the marvellous literature of Socialism, above all with the writings of CHARLES FOURIER. You will doubtless find in Fourier things of an apostolic hardness to the understanding; you will find many things to startle, many things perhaps to disgust you; but you will find vastly more both in the way of criticism and of constructive science to satisfy and invigorate your understanding, while such glimpses will open on every hand of God's ravishing harmonies yet to ensue on earth, that your imagination will fairly ache with contentment, and plead to be let off.

These are what you will find in Fourier, provided you have no secret interest dogging your candor and watching to betray it. Let me also tell you what you will *not* find there. You will find no such defaming thought of God as makes His glory to depend upon the antagonism of His creature's shame. You will find no allegation of an essential and eternal contrariety between man and his creative source. Whatever be FOURIER's errors and faults, this crowning and bottomless infamy by no means attaches to him. On the contrary, if the highest homage paid to Deity be that of the understanding, then FOURIER's piety may safely claim pre-eminence. For it was not a traditional piety, that piety of habit which keeps our churches open—and cheerless; nor was it a selfish piety, the piety which springs from jail-bird conceptions of Deity, and paints him as a colossal spider bestriding the web of destiny and victimizing

with fell alacrity every heedless human fly that
gets entangled in it ; but a piety as broad as human
science, co-extensive in fact with the sphere of his
senses, for its prayers were the passions or wants
of the universal human heart, its praises the laws
or methods of the human understanding, and its
deeds the innumerable forms of spontaneous human
action,

MORALITY

AND

THE PERFECT LIFE.

LECTURE.

———

The subject of the present Lecture, is the relation between man's moral experience and his experience of the divine or perfect life. Two doctrines exist in the world, that of Moralism, which affirms man's rightful subjection to nature and society ; and that of the Christ, or Divine Man, which affirms man's rightful subjection only to God ; and these two are so contrary one to the other as to fill the whole earth with the dust and the noise of their contention. Let us enquire to which of them the eventual triumph is due.

In the four gospels, Christianity or the doctrine of a Divine Natural Humanity, is set forth under a double aspect, a literal and a spiritual one. The

Christ, or Divine Man, claims for himself a double advent, one fleshly and humble, arising from the opposition of nature and society, the other spiritual and glorious, arising from the consent of nature and society. Not only does the Christ challenge to himself this double advent, but he invariably makes the humble one necessary to the glorious one, makes the one an inseparable basis or condition of the other.

If we ask the philosophy of this connection, if we ask the reason why God cannot perfectly reveal Himself in humanity, without first revealing Himself imperfectly; why He cannot reveal Himself in a manner to engage the cordial acknowledgment of society, without first revealing Himself in a manner to provoke its contempt and denial; we shall find ourselves instantly referred to the end or object which God proposes in creation. Of course, when I speak of God as proposing an end to Himself, or as capable of reflective action, you will grant me indulgence, knowing that this is a mere logical necessity, a necessity arising out of the infirmity of our thought, and that I do not mean seriously to ascribe conditions of space and time to the divine action.

The end then which God proposes in creation, is

the communication of Himself to the creature.
This follows from the fact that God is life or being
itself. He does not *possess* being or life. He *is* it.
He *constitutes* it. Consequently in giving being or
life to the creature, he gives Himself to the
creature. God, says Swedenborg, would dwell
in the creature as in Himself. That is to say,
He would be in the creature his very inmost and
vital self, endowing him with a sweetness of affection, with a reach of intellect, and a power of action so spontaneous and infinite as to yield every-
where and always the lavish demonstration of His
presence.

You cannot conceive this point too strictly, for it
is the very corner-stone of a scientific cosmology.
Let me therefore repeat it. Because God is Life
itself, life in its essence, He cannot impart life save
by imparting Himself. He cannot impart it by
transferring it, according to the vulgar conception,
from Himself *to* another, because, inasmuch as He
is life, inasmuch as He constitutes it, this would be
to transfer Himself from Himself, or divide Himself, which is absurd. Creation consequently does
not imply a transfer of life from God Himself to another ; it implies the communication of His integral
or infinite self to another.

But now you will admit that I cannot enjoy this divine communication save in so far as I am prepared for it. I must be a vessel, a form, a subject, receptive of God, before He can communicate Himself to me. If I were destitute of this previous subjectivity, you could not properly say that God communicated Himself to me; you could only say that He transformed or transmuted Himself into me, thus merging the Creator in the creature, and so falsifying both. I must then be a vessel, a house, a tabernacle, a temple, in short a *form*, into which God may come and abide; thus and not otherwise may He be truly said to communicate Himself to me.

But if this be so, if the divine communication to the creature be contingent upon the latter's capacity of reception, then manifestly the process of creation involves or necessitates a two-fold consciousness on the part of the creature; first a finite or imperfect consciousness, or a consciousness of a selfhood distinct from God; and second, an infinite or perfect consciousness, a consciousness of a selfhood united with God. The end of God in my creation is to impart Himself to me, to make Himself over to me with all His infinite resources of love, wisdom, and power. But in order to this end I must first exist, must first have a *quasi* selfhood, a conditional or finite existence, by the medium of which I may become introduced, as it were, to my divine bridegroom, and give myself away in an eternal espousals.

Now a finite or conditional existence is the result of a balance or equilibrium between two opposite forces. All finite experience is generated of opposition. The orbit or individuality of the earth, for example, results from a perfect balance of the repellent and attractive influences of the sun, a perfect equilibrium of its centrifugal and centripetal motions. Destroy either of these motions, and the earth becomes, in the one case, dissipated in space, in the other re-absorbed in the sun. Precisely similar is the genesis of man's finite experience. He becomes self-conscious, self-defined, by the experience of two opposite laws or principles inciting his activity, which laws or principles are variously named, the one external the other internal, the one public the other private, the one evil the other good, the one infernal the other celestial.

The first of these principles is self-love. It answers to the projectile or centrifugal force of nature, and appears to bear the creature away from humanity, away from the centre of human life and

energy ; the relation of the race towards him being
one meanwhile of repulsion. The second law or
force bears the name of charity or benevolence. It
answers to the centripetal force of nature, and appears to bring the creature back again to the heart
of humanity, the relation of the race towards him
being now one of attraction, and this attraction is so
potent that if it were not for the counterbalance
aforesaid, the creature would lose his self-consciousness, and become swallowed up in the race, to the
complete frustration of creation. The operation of
either law unchecked by the other, would be fatal
to the finite consciousness : for the former would
affirm the individual to the denial of the universal,
while the latter would affirm the universal to the
denial of the individual, and these being correlative,
the denial of one is a virtual denial of both.

Man's finite self hood or experience then demands for its perfect development an exact balance
or equilibrium of these two loves, self-love and brotherly love, or charity. As the orbit or individuality of any planet reflects the perfect balance of its
centrifugal and centripetal tendencies, so the or-
bitual or normal life of man reflects the perfect balance of his internal and external self, of charity and
self-love, of good and evil, of heaven and hell.

How then does this finite and preliminary experience of mine become elaborated? What constitutes its apparatus? Nature and society. My experience of the natural and the moral life is what gives me a finite consciousness, a consciousness of a selfhood distinct from every other self. My relations to nature incessantly inspire the sentiment of self-love. My relations to society, or to my fellow man, as incessantly inspire the counter sentiment of charity or brotherly-love. Nature subjects me to the operation of self-love by the various stimulants it offers to my senses, leading me to seek their continual and highest possible gratification. Society, or the fellowship of my kind, subjects me to the equal operation of charity or neighborly love, by the various incitements it offers to my affections, leading me to seek *their* continual and highest possible gratification. My normal state or condition is that which exactly harmonizes or equilibrates these two forces. In the exact ratio of the preponderance of either force over the other, my condition becomes morbid, and my action vicious.

I say that the normal state of man exacts the perfectly balanced or harmonic operation of these principles, because man's perfection as the creature of God requires that he act of himself, or freely and without any impediment *ab extra*. God the creator is infinite or perfect, being sufficient unto Himself. And He is sufficient unto Himself, only because His action is self-generated, or obeys no outward end. This being the case with the creator, and the creature being necessarily only His image or reflection, it follows that the creature must exhibit a like infinitude or perfection. It follows that he also must be sufficient unto himself, or exhibit a purely self-derived activity, an activity which denies any outward motive or impulsion. And the creature cannot exhibit this perfection, this self-sufficiency, so long as either nature or society dominates him, so long as either force exerts a *commanding* influence upon his activity. Whenever this phenomenon occurs consequently, he manifests a diseased or abnormal life, his action being perverted and inhuman.

How then practically, or in point of fact, does this abnormal life of man come about? How does it happen that man, the creature of God, and therefore essentially or inwardly perfect, comes to experience the discordant operation of these laws and to exhibit a consequently infirm activity?

The explanation of this phenomenon lies in the fact that man's perfect or infinite selfhood, that which he derives from God, becomes evolved only by the gradual elimination or removal of his finite self hood, that which he derives from nature and society. While this finite self hood exists in full force, he remains unconscious of his true or infinite one ; and it is only as he puts the former away from him accordingly, only as he eliminates or puts it out of doors, making it merely formal and natural, that the latter flows in and becomes established. Now this process of eliminating the finite selfhood depends altogether upon our experience of its unfitness to satisfy our essential nature. The more vivid and intense the latter experience, the more thorough and consummate will be the consequent process of elimination. All this will become very plain to you after briefly considering the constitution of our finite self hood or experience.

In the first place, Nature gives me a bodily individuality, distinct from all other bodies. Then Society guarantees me an exclusive property or self-hood in this body, gives me a title to its possession good against every other individual. If it were not for the phenomenon of society or fellowship among men, if men were simply gregarious like sheep, then with their tremendous individuality they would soon exterminate each other. First, the strong would exterminate the weak, then the more strong the less strong, until you would finally get down to the solitary strongest man, dismal denizen of the unpeopled planet. It is society then which developes my selfhood or property in my natural body. How does it do this?

By various means. Primarily, by means of the family institution. The domestic guardianship provided for me by society, ensures the care of my infant existence, and the supply of its most urgent wants. Secondly, by means of its municipal and political institutions, which afford me an ampler field of existence than the family supplies, and still further develope my instincts of action. Thirdly, by means of its institutes of education, which enlarge my knowledge of nature and man, and incite me to a proportionately enlarged activity. Thus you perceive that we derive from nature and society a selfhood intrinsically finite, finited successively by our relations to our own body or outlying nature, to our natural progenitors and the inmates of home, to our fellow-townsmen, to our fellow-countrymen, and to the men of other lands.

Such is the constitution of the selfhood we derive from nature and society, inevitably finite or imperfect. First of all it is limited to the body, or the experience of the five senses, shut up as it were to a pin's point in space and time ; and when afterwards through the fostering care of society, it becomes developed and enlarged, it still remains finite, still falls short of its rightful infinitude, of that infinitude which belongs to it by virtue of its creation. For you will admit that society has hitherto done nothing to perfect man. Its institutions have indeed marked an expanding consciousness within him, but the most advanced of them fail to give him perfect enfranchisement, fail to express that relation of perfect unity which he is under to nature and his fellow-man, by virtue of his divine original or source. Let us, for a moment, recount the successive steps of our social progress, and observe when we shall have reached the end, how inadequately society yet serves our true individuality.

Society means fellowship, nothing more and nothing less. A perfect or imperfect society consequently means a perfect or imperfect fellowship among men. But now you know that all true fellowship among men is spontaneous, that it has an inward or spiritual root, instead of an outward or material one. Men may indeed exhibit an *apparent* fellowship with one another while striving to supply their common natural wants ; but this fellowship being outwardly generated or imposed, is only apparent. Each of the parties to it in truth is seeking only to help himself by the aid of the others, and consequently when this end is attained, their friendship is dissolved, and the parties know each other no longer. The present relation of master and servant, of employer and laborer, or of two business partners, illustrates this spurious and evanescent fellowship.

A true fellowship or society then among men has an internal ground or origin, springs from their spontaneous sympathies and attractions. Its foundation is the unity of human nature, a unity which exacts the utmost variety or distinction in the elements composing it. Exactly in the degree in which these various elements become freely asserted, will their unity be manifested, will human society become perfected. The case herein is precisely similar to a musical harmony. The harmony is grand or complete just in the degree that its elemental notes are relatively various and distinct. If the notes are all accordant with each other, the result is at best a simple melody. But if each note gives a distinct sound from every other, then the result is a grand and rapturous harmony that lifts the soul to God. So in human society, if each member be similar in genius, in taste, in action to every other, we have at best a dismal monotony, a mere mush of mutual deference and apology. But if each is distinctively himself, or sharply individualized from every other, then we have a grand choral life hymning the infinitely various graces of the divine unity.

Human society must, therefore, be a very gradual achievment. For the unity which binds man to the race is not an obvious fact, or a fact visible to the senses. It is a fact hidden in God. The fact which is visible to the senses, is the infinite variety of the race. Variety is the only visible form or revelation of unity. We never attain, accordingly, to the realization of unity, until we have first undergone the experience of variety. Hence, before the race realizes its unity, the unity it has in God, it is bound to realize its variety, the variety it has in its own members.

This being the case, our first social forms, the first institutions declarative of our social unity, are of necessity very narrow and imperfect, being based upon a narrow induction of particulars, upon a narrow experience of variety. The distinction of the sexes is the first or most obvious feature of this variety, and furnishes accordingly the basis of our unitary experience, the germ of our unitary consciousness. The *marriage* institution, declaring the union of one man with one woman, is the earliest social form or institution known to the race, and the rudiment of all the others. One man and one woman experience a passional sympathy with each other, which leads them into a complete union, leaving all other men and women out from it. The offspring of this union furnishes the material of the *family* institution, an institution which expresses the union of the children of one married pair, and excludes from it the children of every other pair. These children in their turn each beget families, and the union of these families again gives rise to the *tribal* institution, the tribe being the union of all the families descending from one original family. The tribal union again generates the *town*, or union of many tribes; and the town, in its turn, generates the *nation*, or the union of many towns. Thus all these institutions beginning with marriage, or the union of one man and one woman, and ending with the nation, or the union of many towns, are merely so many enlarging expressions of human unity, developed by our experience of variety. They are so many types or symbols of that internal and integral unity which men have in their Creator; and they take place or result each in its turn from an increasing experience on the part of the race of the infinite variety which characterizes its members.

Now you perceive from this rapid sketch that these various social forms or institutions serve but to finite man, serve but to limit and straiten his infinite personality. While each of them, compared with its predecessor, is an enlarged type of human unity, they are yet all, when compared with that unity itself, most finite and inadequate. Thus, though the family institution expresses a larger unity than the marriage institution, being the union of many brothers and sisters instead of one man and one woman only, yet it is itself finite as limited to the issue of one pair. So the tribal union, though it is a larger type of unity than the family institution, being the union of *many* families, is yet finite as excluding all other tribes. And so forth till we get to the nation, which, while it is a more advanced type of unity than that afforded by the town or municipal institution, is yet itself finite as excluding all other nations. Thus all the social institutions which have yet arisen in the world, and which constitute the existing form or body of society, are, when compared with the great spiritual fact itself, finite or insufficient. They none of them express man's infinite or perfect unity with his fellow. They express the partial, not the universal unity of the race. Thus, at best, they express the unity of the English-man with the English-man and Scotch-man or Irish-man; but in so doing assert his disunion with the French-man and Spanish-man, and so far prove only a partial image of the truth as it is in God.

And as these institutions are thus finite or imperfect, so they engender in their subject a very finite or imperfect consciousness. They impress him with an extreme narrowness, a most incomplete individuality, an individuality which is not charged with the positive virtue of God, but is a mere sickly reflection of these domineering social relations. They teach him that the great end of his existence is to become a good husband, a good brother, a good neighbor and a good citizen. Consequently they propose a continually finite righteousness to him, and fill him with conceit in the exact ratio of his attainments.

But man being above all things the creature of God, feels the inward intimation and prophecy of a larger unity with his fellow than these institutions affirm or allow, even a *perfect* unity, which these institutions deny. The consequence is a conflict between man and existing institutions, between humanity and society.   Thus the marriage-subject, finding himself in spiritual relation or relations of affection with some other person than his legal partner, is led to violate the marriage obligation. So the family-subject, finding himself in closer spiritual accord, in relations of superior friendship with other families than his own, is led practically to disesteem and transcend that tie.   So, also, the citizen, coming into relations of greater amity and sympathy with other nations than his own, learns to renounce his national allegiance.   In all these cases you perceive that the evil arises not from the spirit of humanity, but from the imperfection of the institutions which profess to embody that spirit. Man is spiritually larger than the institutions which pretend to contain him.   He consequently over-flows their boundaries and exposes them to contempt.

This is the true philosophy of crime.   It arises from an antagonism between the spirit of humanity, or what is the same thing the divine spirit in man, and existing social institutions.   Take away this antagonism and you immediately exhaust crime. Let society become perfectly expressive of humanity, let its institutions reflect the unity of the race, and instantly universal love would abound, and

what is better, a love which would be without reflective consciousness, without self-complacency,
without a sense of merit.

The divine spirit in every man incessantly urges
his unity with nature and his fellow man, his unity
with the universe. Thus, if you regard the child
before he becomes morally sophisticate, or disciplined by society, you perceive that he views all
things and all persons as made for his delight, and
puts forth his hand with a lordly disdain of every
laborious distinction of *meum* and *tuum*. Now the
child is but the prophecy of the man. His ignorant
innocence only typifies that wiser innocence which
shall endow and render beautiful the ripe divine
manhood. Hence the Christ affirmed that we
should enter the kingdom of heaven only by becoming as little children, that is, by putting away those
vain subtilties of philosophy which base our present
diseased manhood, and subjecting ourselves with
the candor of children to the infallible laws of
God.

But, however this may be, it is evident to you
from the past rapid sketch, that society has thus far
done nothing for the individual but to deepen or
intensify his moral consciousness, that is, to bring
him under law successively to his wife, his children,

his relatives, his neighbors, his fellow countrymen. The most it has done for him is to allow him a relative goodness, a goodness lying in his relations to other people.   But clearly, man should be good by virtue of his creation, or his relation to the infinite God, should be good in himself, infinitely good.   It is impossible either that God's creature should be evil in himself, or derive goodness from any other source than his creator.   The former position obviously stultifies itself.   And to suppose the creature's goodness flowing from any other source than the creator, as from his relation to other creatures, is to make the original goodness, of which it is only an image, also flow not from God Himself, but from His relations to other beings.   It is, in short, to make God's goodness contingent instead of positive.

Hence society has failed hitherto perfectly to subserve the interests of human individuality.   It has given the individual expansion, but only in a downward or subversive direction, such an expansion as you give the prisoner, not by breaking his chains and bidding him be free, but by enlarging and multiplying the wards of his prison.   Consequently you perceive what you have every *a priori* warrant to anticipate, that individual history has presented little else hitherto than a warfare between nature and society, between self-love and charity. Nature and society having themselves no individuality are utterly godless, exhibit no faintest suspicion of man's vital source. Accordingly they suggest to him only an outward law of action, only an outward principle of development : the former, the law of self-love, the law of his relation to his own body ; the latter the law of charity, the law of his relation to his fellow-man. Nature bids him realize his infinitude, his perfection, by the service of his own body. Society bids him realize it by the service of his fellow-man. Thus neither nature nor society conceives it to be already provided and secure in God, and only waiting the cessation of their strife to flow into his consciousness ; but regards it on the other hand as a thing to be assiduously coaxed out of their own costive and innutritious udders.

The individual thus disciplined consequently, and feeling in every pulse of his soul the instinct of sovereignty, proceeds to realize it by these natural and moral methods. If he be of an external or sensuous genius, he pursues the former method, the method of pleasure, obeying the law of self-love. If he be of an inward and reflective temper, he pursues the latter method, the method of duty, obeying the law of brotherly love. But the more diligently he prosecutes either pursuit, that of pleasure or this of duty, the further he strays from his great quest and accumulates defeat. For his freedom is not his own laborious achievment, it is the cordial gift of God. It does not come to him in any outward way, from any service however zealous either of necessity or duty. It comes to him in a purely inward and supersensuous way as a perpetual influx from God into his soul. While he seeks therefore to wring it out of the base reluctant bowels of nature and society, while he seeks, in short, anything with them but to compel them into the speediest and fullest possible imagery or reflection of it, it perpetually baffles his grasp, and beats him to the dust in shame and despair.

For suppose him to succeed never so well in either of these paths. Suppose him, for example, to accumulate never so much of the bounties of nature. Then just in proportion to that accumulation will be his care, his anxiety, his painful servitude. Instead of realizing his freedom he loses it. He has less of it now than he had when he stood naked under God's sky, with nought to shield him from the giant sport of nature. For what he has gained will only stay gained on condition of his continually adding to it. Every day consumes it, and every day therefore puts forth new claims upon his relentless toil. Thus having once entered upon this service, he finds no release till he has conquered all nature, made all her resources his own; and this nature herself denies him force to do.

Or suppose him to gain never so much of the esteem of his fellow-man, and to abound in all manner of moral excellence. Now just in proportion to his abundance in this direction also, will be his care, his anxiety, his painful servitude. For moral goodness does not stay of its own momentum. It stays only upon the condition of continual augmentation. If I say "I denied myself and was good yesterday; to-day therefore I will take my ease and enjoy myself;" that yesterday's goodness instantly perishes, and I am obliged to begin clean anew. No, the more earnestly I strive to achieve moral goodness, to fulfil the law of brotherly love, the more I find incessantly to do, the less hope of release have I in time or eternity. For this law is spiritual, demanding in the votary a mind of perfect equality with every other man, and therefore mortally inimical to the aspirations of individual ambition. The only man who fulfils it, the only man who, in

fact, fulfils either law, the law of self-love or
of neighborly love, the law of nature or of society, is the divine or perfect man, the man who
asks nothing either of nature or of his fellow-man,
because He already has all things in God, and whom
therefore both nature and society hasten to glorify
and adore.

Now this experience on the part of man of the
utter vanity of his pursuits, of the utter inability
both of nature and society to satisfy his aspiration
and give him peace with himself, although bitterly
painful in its transit, has yet the most indispensable
uses in convincing him of his essential infinitude,
and leading him to disown and reject the finite selfhood. If it were not for the perpetual disappoint-
ment he encounters in the pursuit both of pleasure
and righteousness, he would sink into the abject
tool or votary of nature and his fellow-man, and the
immortal instinct he derives from God would expire
consequently with the decay of nature and the dis-
ruption of his social ties. But these disappoint-
ments nurse his infinitude, conserve his immortality.
They guard the interests of his unconscious destiny,
giving it an invincible development and relief. Re-
fusing utterly to satisfy his instinct of sovereignty,
ministering his most impassioned solicitations only
the ashes of disease and death, they throw him in-

cessantly and perforce upon his inward self, and
teach him to ask life where alone it may be found
without money and without price, in the divine and
unfathomable depths of his own spontaneous nature.

For here is the birth of Art, or the true divine
life in man. Art is nothing else than the obedience
of one's spontaneous tastes or attractions, uncontrolled either by nature or society, by necessity
or duty. And this obedience would be forever impossible to man, if nature or society gave him
repose, if they met and appeased the cry of his soul
for freedom. If nature perfectly satisfied me, if society perfectly justified me ; if my relations to the
one brought me no consciousness of disease, and my
relations to the other no consciousness of sin ; then
I should be forever content to feed upon honey, and
bask in the smile of my fellows, ignoring God, ignoring destiny. But as neither satisfies or justifies me,
as my addiction to nature or self-love convinces me
only of disease and death, and my addiction to society or duty convinces me only of sin; so I am incessantly driven inwards upon myself, upon my
own spontaneous tendencies and attractions, which
are the throne of God's power and majesty, to rea-

lize an infinite righteousness, or a self hood at perfect harmony with man and nature.

I have now shewn you what I engaged to shew
you, namely, how the realization of man's destiny
or perfection involved not only his experience of a
finite self hood, but also his gradual renunciation of
it—his complete elimination of it or putting it out of
doors, there to stand and wait upon his infinite one.
Doubtless many questions occur to you hereupon,
which I have not now the space and time to answer.
Let us postpone these to future occasions, when the
same impediments will not exist, and proceed now
to the confirmation and illustration of what has been
already said.

It is clearly deducible then from all I have said,
that I hold morality to be a transient phenomenon
of humanity, or to pertain only to man's immature
experience, having not only no relevancy to him as
the creature of God, but imposing a positive disability upon that relation. I beg that no one will be
silly enough to charge me hereupon with maintain-
ing that our consciousness of unity with God will
involve a continued consciousness of hostile relations with nature or man. On the contrary, I hold
the activity of the latter consciousness to be altogether contingent upon the dormancy of the former

one, and that nothing accordingly is needed for the utter abolition of our present vicious relations with nature, and criminal relations with man, than the recognition of our unity with God. It is exclusively our infidelity towards God which leaves us under the tyranny of nature and society, and we have only to acknowledge the truth as to the former and higher relation, to find this tyranny perfectly innocuous, to find it in fact transformed into a complete and measureless benediction.

I know very well the prestige which surrounds existing institutions. I know the tremendous grasp which the existing form of society has upon our imagination and I should be utterly hopeless of every attempt to weaken it, did I not feel assured that the whole force of divine Providence, the total movement of human destiny, co-operated with such attempts. Its institutions are effete. The vigorous life which once gave them repute has departed. They no longer bless the subject. To be a good husband, a good brother, a good neighbor, a good citizen, is no longer a guarantee against starvation. For one that society feeds and clothes it sends ten thousand naked and empty away. For one it fills with the vapid froth of self-conceit, it fills ten thousand with an unappeasible consciousness of want and sin. To save appearances it hastens indeed to trip up the heels of the burglar, and immure the petty thief in prison. But it *organizes* the systematic pillage of the stock exchange, and builds up the fortune of its rich men upon the actual murder of its poor. It proclaims from all its pulpits the undiminished terrors of the devil, and the lake of fire and brimstone, but with what effect? He to whom the tidings might be profitable, the selfish man, laughs with incredulity; and only they to whom they are wholly irrelevant, the tender-hearted woman and the man of gentle affections, drag out a life of miserable uncertainty, or else renounce it in violent despair. Will God endure this?

Society was made for man, not man for society. It is the steward of God not His heir, and He holds it therefore to a rigid accountability. If it regards the interests of the heir in the first place accordingly, and its own interests in the second place, then He will bestow upon it abundant honor; *it shall reflect in fact all the glory of the heir*. But if it forget its intrinsic subordination or stewardship, and claim to be itself the heir, He will deprive it even of this reflected glory, and deliver it over to contempt and death.

But this has been the capital mistake of society

from the beginning. The heir has so long delayed his coming, that the steward has grown bold and come to look upon himself as the heir. So obdurate has this conviction waxed, that it apparently requires every arrow in God's quiver to arouse him from his delusion. Nothing else explains the present stupidity of society under the desolating judgments which are visiting it. It seems to have utterly abjured that purely secondary or ministerial place to man which it occupies in the divine regard. It believes itself valued by God for its own sake, and not for its worth to the individual soul, that soul whose existence in nature would be impossible without it. It esteems itself a true divine end, and not merely a means to that end, and thus perpetually antagonizes the Divine Humanity, the spirit of God in man, exerting an implacable tyranny over the individual life.

But man *cannot* succumb to this tyranny. He may not be able to justify his resistance intellectually, he may not be able to cast back the reproach of society into its own teeth, but he will not suffer it to compress his passions with impunity. They will burst forth upon occasion with destructive energy—an energy *whose destructiveness however refers itself purely to that foregone compression*—and assert their divine and imperishable freedom, if not in a positive or orderly way, still in a manner to show the perfect impotence of society to subdue them.

Talk as you will, society remains stupidly deaf. Taking her stand upon her existing institutions, she deals out her vindictive anathema upon every one who practically refuses to be contained in them. She never suspects that the cause of the disobedience she encounters lies in these very institutions themselves, in their finiteness, in their refusal to expand with the expansion of God's life in man. Because they have been good in the past, because each in its turn was a larger type of human unity than its predecessor, society regards them also as final, or as constituting the substance of that unity. It is as though this temporary body of mine should assume to live after the spirit had departed from it, should presume upon my spirit's eternity because of its use to that spirit in time. Doubtless my body has been helpful to my spirit, but there comes a period to this relation, a period when the body has attained its climax of experience, and no longer promotes but actually hinders the growth of my spirit. For the service it has rendered me I no doubt owe it decent burial. But whether decent or

7

indecent, burial is its infallible doom, burial out of human sight, and resolution into elemental nature.

Exactly such is the fate of all our social institutions. None of them is adequate fully to express man's spiritual unity, since the only adequate expression of that is the organization of the whole race in perfect fellowship, an organization not by human legislation, not by police, not by convention, but by God's legislation which is SCIENCE, and primarily by that method of science which has been termed *the law of the series,* and applied to the human passions. Our present institutions, at least all those which vitalize our morality blink this inward or spiritual unity of the race. They proceed upon a certain outward and natural unity, as that of persons born under one roof, or in one vicinage, or in one country. But they have no eye for that spiritual unity which disdains the limitations of space and time, and gives the whole race the continuity of a man, the integrity of God. Accordingly, as this spiritual unity asserts itself more and more in human consciousness, it more and more disowns the old institutions, and craves forms proportionate to itself.

Thus you perceive that the march of the divine Providence in the earth incessantly demands the enlargement of existing institutions, their enlargement or their overthrow. If the established forms obstinately resist the new life, if they will not expand with the expansion of the individual genius, it is manifest that they have survived their use, and only encumber the earth. I do not say that the divine life finds its *normal* or positive manifestation in methods of violence, for that life is essential peace and all its paths are those of pleasantness. But when society puts itself in antagonism with man, when it gathers itself up in its present embankments and refuses to enlarge itself to the dimensions of universal humanity, then the divine Providence must needs ally itself with those whom society thus drives to violence and turbulence. What God is bound to hate, what He is bound by His every perfection to disallow, is the attempt of society to organize permanent division among His children, those children whom He unites. Hence His earliest manifestations in nature must of necessity bear a hostile aspect towards society, or towards every institution which gives one class of men a permanent superiority over others.

From this exposition you will have no difficulty in perceiving why God's first revelation of Himself in humanity takes place under circumstances of humiliation, or provokes the contempt of the devout

and polite world, of all the friends of the existing
order. It is because it is necessarily hostile to that
order, because God cannot affirm the insane pretension of society to the supremacy over man, but
on the contrary would have it totally subordinate
to him. If the divine man, the man of genius, the man
of inward force, the man of ideas, in short the Artist,
would succumb to society ; if he would say nothing
and do nothing which society disallowed, nothing
subversive of its customs and traditions; if he would
utter no prophecies and confess no want of a superior
righteousness to that which flowed from the obedience of existing institutions ; then society would
gladly honor him, and give him the pomp and glory
of all the kingdoms of the world.

But the Artist is unable to gratify society in this
thing. He lives from God alone, from the inspirations of truth and beauty in his own soul, and he
cannot acknowledge any law or institution which
limits these. Hence in an immature or dissentient
society his lot is to suffer outwardly, to be crucified
in the flesh even while he is being glorified in the
spirit, even in order to his being thus glorified. Accordingly, if you will search history through, you
will find the divine life asserting itself in man always under social obstruction and contempt. No

man of ideas ever announced himself without arous-
ing the fanatic jealousy of society, without its chief
priests and rulers predicting disaster, and stirring
up the populace to his destruction. But the divine
life is never quenched. The very dungeon to
which it is shut up becomes a radiant centre of
energy to it, and the gallows only a more conspicuous witness of its immortality.

But you need not career over the whole of history
to learn these things. You are Christians from your
youth up, instructed in the literal doctrine of the
Christ from your mothers' breasts, and I am only
setting before you the spirit of that doctrine as it
glows and burns in the sacred letter. You know
that it was just this conflict which was enacted between the Jew and the Christ. Perhaps your teach-
ers have failed to tell you that the Christ had
never any quarrel with the individual as absolved
from social unity, but only with society, only with
the rulers of the nation in church and state. The
individual who stood absolved from social unity,
who was cast out for his unworthiness, had no word
of condemnation from those guileless lips : publicans and sinners believed his quarrel just, and the
common people, we are told, heard him gladly.

But the un-common people, they who were iden-

tified with the national honor, the scribe and Pharisee, and high priest and elder of the people, the
person, in short, who prized his Judaism above his
humanity, he it was with whom Christ's quarrel lay.
The Jew took his stand upon the national righteousness, upon the ground of his national difference
from other men, exhibited in his exemplary fulfilment of all the duties of his law, and on this ground
challenged the divine acceptance and favor. You
know that the Christ systematically gainsaid this
pretension, that he refused to admit the slightest superiority in the Jew over the Gentile, the saint over
the sinner, that he consequently incurred the tem-
pestuous scorn and enmity of the nation, but that
he never ceased to denounce them as hypocrites
and liars, children of the devil, whose damnation
was irresistible and everlasting. You know that
he proclaimed himself the friend of publicans and
sinners, the herald of God not to the righteous but
to sinners, the physician of the sick not of the well.
You know that he denied the divine kingdom to be
of this world, or to be modelled upon the fashion of
any existing society, a kingdom that is in which
one should be exalted and another despised, one
rich and another poor, one powerful another weak.
In short you know that he represented the righteous-

ness of that kingdom as entirely superior to that
of the Scribes and Pharisees, being a righteousness
which should invest all its subjects equally, and
obliterate every conventional difference of good and
evil, by satisfying every soul with fatness.

Now, my friends, these things have happened for
our instruction, upon whom the ends of the world
have truly come. Is any one here silly enough to
believe that the Jew is one outwardly, or that the
true Judæa with which the Christ contends, belongs to a peculiar geographical latitude, and not to
human nature ? If so, my friend, you have managed to preserve a very placid bosom in the midst
of great disquiets. You have managed, in fact, to
stagnate in the very heart of universal movement.
But this is a rare case. To most men Judæa is a
bosom experience. For my own part, I very much
fear that I might not be able on the instant to define
the exact geographical Judæa to you, yet I should
have no suspicion of my particular exclusion from
God's vital drama. But Judæa, which is ungeo-
graphical, Judæa which is spiritual and represents
ideas, this Judæa we all carry about with us in our
souls, and daily reproduce in all the features of its
deathless personality.

I admit that the literal Judæa was once a great

fact. I admit that it esteemed itself and aspired to be as no nation ever aspired to be, the chosen and appropriate inheritance of God. I admit that it came into collision with the literal Christ, or representative Divine Man, and that it was bound by every consideration of a puny patriotism, and every interest of a cruel morality, to put him to a bloody death. But now remember that after death there comes a resurrection. We may say, indeed, that death is only in order to a resurrection, that it is merely a transition point between lower and higher, between less life and more life. For example, you put the seed in the ground : it dies, it rots, it disappears, but out of that death, that corruption, that disappearance springs a plant, a flower or fruit which shall fill the earth with plenty, with beauty, with joy. Thus the literal Christ has passed away : never again shall we behold him after the flesh or finitely. The literal Judæa has also tasted death : nevermore shall its altars smoke, nor the sound of tabor and pipe enliven its streets. But both Judæa and the Christ have a spiritual resurrection or glorification : Judæa in the ideas and institutions of our modern civilization ; the Christ in all those instincts of freedom, in all those aspirations after peace, after harmony, after joy, after the unimpeded exercise of

one's faculties of action, which are subtly but irre-
sistibly laying that civilization law.

I have a perfect faith that Christianity had never
such vitality on earth as now, that all those great
events which occurred under Herod and Pontius
Pilate were, in fact, only figurative of the transcen-
dent realities in which we now live and act. The
controversy of the Christ with the Jew, and his delivery by the Jew into the hands of the Roman, only
symbolize the present injustice which the interests
of human individuality encounter at the hands of
the Church, and the interested sycophancy of the
latter towards the State, or secular power. One
gets tired of witnessing the barren idolatry of Jesus,
an idolatry which consists with the habitual profanation of every truth he uttered and put into life ;
tired of hearing him called Lord! Lord! while as
yet we obey every influence to which he gave his
life a sacrifice. For my own part, I seek to know
the Christ no more after the flesh, no more in his
finite and perishable form. I seek to know him
henceforth only in his second or infinite and universal manifestation, as the power of God in *every* individual soul. The sphere of God is the soul of universal humanity, and His highest revelation is in
the individual life. A perfect life, a life that is

7*

whose every act and word are true to the sovereign
soul within, will ever be the truest revelation of
God, as it is the highest expression of Art.

When Jesus Christ amidst the dripping scorn of
all the devout minds of his nation, outspake the
measureless kindness with which his heart was
aglow towards the woman taken in adultery : when
he confronted the dignitaries of his people, those
who were esteemed by all his friends and neighbors as eminently the servants of God, and pro-
nounced them mere actors or hypocrites, children
of their father the devil : when he met the obtru-
sive and self-complacent interference of his mother
by the stern rebuke, " Woman, what have I to do
with *thee* ?" when finally feeling in his deepest soul
the shallowness and vanity of these merely natural
ties, he said to those who told him that his mother
and brethren stood without desiring to speak with
him, that " he had no mother nor brethren but such
as did the will of God :" he, in all these cases, only
typified that supreme and beautiful life which is
yet to reveal itself in every man. He indeed exhibited the divine or perfect man under humiliation,
under the obscuration of warring circumstances.
His life did not *seem* beautiful, because the common
or established life was so false as to turn his into an

incessant protest, an incessant warfare. But it was
at bottom the most beautiful and sovereign life ever
exhibited on earth. He alone, of all the race of
men, has dared to be exactly true to his own soul,
or God within him. When I find it so hard for myself to decline an invitation to some paltry tea-party,
for fear of offending the customs of society ; when I
feel it a severe trial to forego the empty and expen-
sive mummery of mourning, lest some infinitesimal
moralist be shocked ; when I hide my hands between my knees at the opera lest Mrs. Grundy
should discover their destitution of an orthodox cov-
ering ; when I huddle away my cards on a Sunday
evening for fear of the neighboring clergyman coming in and finding me at whist with my children ;
the contrast I am thus made aware of between him
and me, leaves me little doubt of his divinity.

He seems, indeed, the only man in history. All
other men seem but lackeys. For the peculiarity
of Christ's manhood, the very divinity of his manli-
ness, was this, that he opposed the best virtue of
his time, and finally fell a victim to it. Unlike the
moralist he despised the cheap fame which flows
from the condemnation of vice and crime. He had
least of all men any relish for vice or crime ; but he
never failed on any occasion to justify the criminal.

I cannot find in all my persevering search of the gospels, an instance in which the Christ was found exalting himself above the blackest sinner. He seems to have had no outward sanctity of any sort. He ate and drank so like the common herd, that they whose righteousness very largely consisted in oddities of diet and other ritual whimsicalities, were fain to consider him gluttonous and a wine-bibber. I find no instance in all his history, in which he ever did a stroke of work whereby to gain a living. On the contrary, so far as *any* light is shed upon the question, he seems to have preferred living by the free-will charity of his followers, some elderly women being incidentally designated as those who ministered to him of their substance. Not a single word is reported of his devout observance of the Sabbath, but on the contrary he is described as profaning it to the popular estimation by doing things upon it which were commonly thought unlawful. And finally he did not hesitate to declare that the kingdom promised in so many words to his people by their sacred prophets, a kingdom over the whole earth, should never be theirs, thus setting himself in direct and glaring opposition to the whole obvious scope of their scriptures.

I see not, for my own part, how the respectable

and orderly classes among the Jews could have acted otherwise than they did with Jesus. I see not, indeed, how we shall be able to justify the Christ historically upon any of the current maxims of morality. It seems to me that if he were to re-appear in our day, we should be bound to regard him as menacing the peace of society. For though he should himself infringe no statute of the moral law, yet if, whilst avowedly acting in the name of God, he should say to the criminal whom we condemn to imprisonment and death, " *I* do not condemn thee, go and sin no more," we should feel that he was gainsaying the deepest principles of the prevailing ethics, and tacitly rebuking our most hallowed institutions.

I am indeed well aware that the Christ is commonly reputed to have been a zealous friend of the current morality. I know very well that he is commonly represented to have come not for the purpose of fulfilling the law by the introduction of a better righteousness than the law itself conferred, but of re-enacting it in an intensely aggravated form. And it is easy to see how this fallacious representation has come about. The great controversy between Jesus and the Jew was as to the true divine man, or the righteousness which stood approved in

God's sight. The Jew contended that it was the man who was blameless in all the national righteousness, in all the righteousness required by the law of Moses. Very well, replied Jesus, but a law to be fulfilled truly must be fulfilled in the spirit as well as the letter. Now as the whole spirit of Moses' law is love to God and love to the neighbor, if you do not in your hearts love your neighbors as yourselves, but on the ground of your superior literal sanctity assume airs over them, it is quite manifest that you miss the whole spirit of the law and stand condemned by your own standard. It is no evidence, therefore, he argued, of a divine man that he zealously obeys the literal enactments of the law. Every thing depends upon the spirit with which this obedience is rendered, whether with a spirit of love to the neighbor, or with a spirit of self-exaltation. He alone truly fulfils the law who regards it not as a task imposed by an outward authority, and with a view therefore to its rewards, but with an inward delight as breathing the divinest and most universal love. It justifies no man but him who does its works for their own sake alone, and not as a means to his own spiritual distinction above other men ; who does them not because he may thus commend himself to the divine favor, but only because of their intrinsic consonance with his own profoundest life. In a word, he who truly fulfils the law, must do it *from* life, and not *to* life ; must do it spontaneously, and not from a mere sense of obligation.

Now, the obvious force of these sayings of Jesus is to rebuke the pride of morality, to abase the vanity of those who conceive that God recognises the paltry differences of human character and feels Himself bound therefore to accord the saint a superior favor to the sinner. He denies that the law was ever intended to be a minister of righteousness. He denies that it had the least power to confer righteousness. He affirms, and his apostles affirm more fully after him, that the law had no other purpose than the *manifestation of evil in its votary.* It was given to its subject as a mirror, wherein beholding himself in his natural and social imperfections, he might be stimulated to aspire after a perfect life. The Jew, indeed, abused this mirror. That is to say he used it for no other purpose than to inflame his vanity. You would say that I abused my looking-glass, if I appealed to it every morning not for the purpose of discovering and removing the disorders of my person, but only for the purpose of proving my personal superiority to other men. Just so did the Jew abuse the looking-glass of the law. Instead of appealing to it to know wherein he fell short of the divine or perfect man, that thus he might go on unto all perfection, he appealed to it to reveal wherein he was superior to other men, namely, the publicans and sinners around him.

Christ admitted that the Pharisee greatly excelled the publicans in legal obedience, but, at the same time denied that this was the appropriate use of the law. This incidental distinction which the law made between the Pharisee and the publican, or the saint and the sinner, was not the great end of the law, any more than the incidental distinction which the looking-glass makes between the handsome and the ugly face is the great design of the looking-glass. The design of the looking-glass is to discover any casual deviations from the dictates of a correct taste which may be exhibited in our outward appearance, and thus subserve the ends of perfect beauty; and any man, therefore, who seeks it not with the view of amendment exclusively, but only with the view of felicitating himself on his manifest superiority to this, that, and the other individual, perverts it from its true end to the service of his own paltry vanity. So the design of the law was only to discover and make plain the numerous infirmities and defects which belong to the natural and social man, the man who is in bondage to nature and society, and thus prepare the way for the divine or perfect man, the man who should perfectly image God. Whenever the Jew therefore sought the law, not for the purpose of discovering wherein he failed of this ideal or perfect man, and thus aspiring more and more after him, but only for the purpose of ascertaining his comparative superiority to other imperfect men, he perverted the law from its divine end, and made it the minister of his own spiritual conceit.

In order to convince the Jew of his error in thus perverting the law, the Christ followed precisely the same course that you would follow, in order to convince the dandy of *his* error in perverting the looking-glass. If you saw him returning every day from the looking-glass with an increased complacency in his own beauty, and an increased contempt accordingly for other men, you would intensify the power of the glass, you would give it a magnifying power, that thenceforth whenever the deluded mortal looked into it, he might discover all those latent seams, wrinkles and blemishes which lie embedded in every skin, and so cease from the idolatry of his stupid face. Just so the Christ intensified

the power of the law, that it might reveal to its votary all those latent seams, wrinkles and blemishes
which inwardly defile his best morality, and so
shame him out of his importunate self-idolatry.
From the depths of his own inmost soul he evoked
the spiritual force or meaning of the law, in order
that he who had hitherto found life in its superficial
letter, might find in its deepest spirit an utter death
to all his conceited hopes and pretensions.

Now our theologians have utterly mistaken all
these sayings of Jesus. Instead of representing
this conduct of his as designed to teach the folly of
the Jew in being satisfied with a merely finite or
comparative righteousness, when he might enjoy an
infinite or positive one by unity with God in his
own soul, they represent it as designed to organize
another law of incomparably deadlier force than the
old one, and to put all men on its vain obedience,
only to magnify his own indispensable importance to
them. Such jugglery and self-seeking men do not
hesitate to ascribe to the purest life in history !

The Jew was, at least, outwardly righteous, as
the Christ allowed. He had some, though an imperfect ground of hope towards God, and felt therefore something of a filial and human relation to Him.
But the Christian according to our theologians is

destitute of all hope towards God both inwardly and outwardly. Two laws are given him to obey, an inward and an outward one, and he cannot possibly obey either. Consequently he must look to another to obey it for him, and so be kept at an infinite and eternal remove from the great source of his life. Thus this divine man who was revealed as a messenger of great joy to all people, even those who sit in the region and shadow of death, who was revealed as the mediator of a universal righteousness which should envelope every creature of God in its sheltering embrace, is habitually palmed off upon us not as the minister or mediator of this righteousness, *but as its substitute*, so that we who are looking for the gift he promised are to be forever satisfied with the mere promise itself. If we go into our synagogues on Sunday, or take up any of the innumerable tracts which like a plague of lice devour the land, we shall hear the Christ held forth not as the pledge and first fruits of a righteousness which shall one day be all men's, but only as a more terrific Moses imposing duties which are utterly impracticable to every truly living soul, and consigning young men and maidens to irreversible perdition for the ineffable offence of frequenting the ball-room and theatre!

But we must all allow that the theatre has had very divine uses. When we contemplate the influence of the prevalent sectarianism, how it weighs like a night-mare upon the soul of man, treading its sweetest blossoms in the dust, and turning its most poetic impulses into a reproach, we cannot help blessing the great Friend of man for the antagonistic influence of the theatre, and the potent charm it yields to human life even in its present rude development.

The ecclesiastical theory of Christianity is a sheer imposition. It has nothing in its favor but the purse and the sword, those two weapons by which society still contrives to maintain its usurpation. It wars with the letter of scripture, with the spirit of the Christ himself, with the developments of history and the universal instincts of the human heart. It would not have a friend or apologist to-morrow, if man were delivered to-day from the bondage of his fellow-man, that is to say, if society instead of seeking to crush the individual beneath itself, vouchsafed to him that plenitude alike of natural subsistence and social respect which the bare fact of his birth in nature and society entitles him to.

But let us return to the consideration of our moral experience.

We have seen that morality marks a very imperfect development of the individual life. The individual life in order to its perfection, exacts a perfect balance of the natural and social law, the law of self-love and the law of charity, a perfect equilibrium in other words between man's appetites and his affections or sympathies. While this balance or equilibrium is yet unattained the individual oscillates between the two extremes, now obeying this law, now obeying that. Morality expresses just this fact of oscillation. It expresses the vibratory or pendulous condition of the human individuality, preparatory to its true and immortal poise or rest in God. Accordingly when the individual obeys the social law, the law of charity, to the denial of the natural law or the law of self-love, we pronounce his morality good, we call him a morally good man. When, on the other hand, he obeys the latter law to the denial of the former, we pronounce his morality evil, calling him a morally evil man. Thus morality always implies a conflict in the subject between the two laws of his finite consciousness. It would be utterly impossible without such conflict. If charity or the social law dictated nothing contrary to self-love or the natural law, then I should never defer to my neighbor, and consequently would dis-

claim all moral goodness.   And if self-love or the
natural law prompted no infringement of charity or
the social law, I should never exalt myself above
my neighbor, and so would disclaim all moral evil.

Morality then is conditioned upon a conflict or antagonism between nature and society, between self-
love and charity, between my natural inclination and
my social sympathies.   When I practically subject
my natural inclinations or appetites to my social
sympathies you pronounce me a good man ; when
I practically subject the latter to the former, you
pronounce me an evil man.

Or let me state the same truth in larger characters.   Morality is conditioned upon an antagonism
between the private and public elements in humanity, upon a conflict between me and the race, between myself and some other self.   Accordingly, I
am either morally good or morally evil, as I practically abase myself to others, or practically exalt
myself above them.

Clearly, then, morality expresses a very imperfect
development of the individual life, such a development as exhibits the individual still in subjection
to nature or society.   It does not characterize
man's perfect individuality, that which he derives from God alone, and which presupposes the

complete reconciliation of nature and society, or self-love and charity. The divine or perfect man, the Artist, ignores both these principles of action. He acts with no view to benefit himself or to benefit others, but simply to express his own delight, to embody his own conception of beauty. Of course it is requisite in order to his doing this, that he be in amicable relation both with nature and man, or that his physical and social subsistence be sure. Because until these conditions be fulfilled, he cannot give diligent heed to the inspirations of God in his soul, but must find himself forever drawn aside to fight with his circumstances.

In thus making morality to characterize our imperfect development, I do not intend to dishonor it, or deny it a true historic function. I hold it to have been both an inevitable and desirable feature of human experience. For our true individuality involves the complete lordship or dominion of nature. But you have only to glance at the universality of nature, to see how impossible it would be for the individual to attain to its lordship or mastery without the aid of his fellow-man, or society. Society, then, as guaranteeing man his lordship or dominion over nature, exerts a powerful claim upon his allegiance, upon his grateful regard. And if man resist this claim,

if he obey the prompting of nature to the denial of
the social claim, he justly incurs the reproach of
evil-doing.   He acts in this case just as the planet
would act which should obey its centrifugal impulse
to the denial of its centripetal one.   As the planet
would, in so doing, become dissipated in space,
thus forfeiting its individuality, so the man who
obeys nature or self-love to the denial of society
or brotherly love, would become immersed in nature, sunken in mere brutality, so forfeiting his
human individuality.   Society, therefore, is a necessary corrective force to that of nature in its operation upon the human individuality.   It serves the
same use precisely to the individual as the centripetal or attractive force of nature does to the planet,
that is, giving him a continual reaction against nature, and so preventing the otherwise inevitable
absorption of his individuality.

Let our moral history have its due honor therefore, as a true development, but let it never be looked upon as a final development, as the consummation of human destiny.   Such an idea would be in
the last degree opprobrious to God and man.   Certainly no Christian should tolerate it for a moment,
for it covers every word and work of the Christ with
mockery and derision.   He declared the divine

forgiveness of all sin, of all moral defilement. Now
as it is incredible that God should tolerate or forgive
any contrariety to his own nature, the inference from
this declaration of the Christ considered as a true
divine herald, is, that our moral delinquencies exhibit no such contrariety, but merely a falling short
of the divine image. They must be a falling short of
this image, otherwise they would not *need* forgiveness. And they cannot imply a contrariety
to it, otherwise they would not *receive* forgiveness.

We cannot deny this inference, and still admit
the truth of Christianity. The whole scope of the
doctrine of the Christ proceeds upon the assumption
of man's redemption from the bondage of nature
and his fellow-man, into the sole subjection of God.
All manner of sin, he said, against the Father and
the Son should be forgiven; but the sin against the
Holy Spirit should not be forgiven either in this
world or the coming one. It is as if he said, "man
may exhibit any want of conformity to the divine
Love or the divine Wisdom; that is, may be very
selfish in heart and very stupid in intellect; and his
destiny remain unaffected. But he cannot resist the
divine Power, or Inspiration, in his own soul without utter defeat to the end of his creation." Accord-

ing to this doctrine, the only sin for man which
God cognizes is the sin against the Holy Spirit, or
the resistance of his own genius, and this, thank
God, is a sin which no individual is capable of committing.   Both nature and society may prevent me
following my genius, may keep it completely latent
and undiscovered, by holding me in incessant bondage to themselves, but while God remains supreme
they cannot make me actually resist it.   Insanity
or suicide would speedily decide that controversy in my favor.

The practical conclusion of the whole matter is,
my friends, that we should cease to hold the individual accountable for his moral delinquencies.   We
should give up the indolent and futile habit of
blaming the thief, the liar, the adulterer, the drunk-
ard for their abominations, and place the blame
where alone it truly belongs, upon our defective
social organization.   Should a planet fly from its
orbit and become dispersed in space, you might
with exactly the same propriety hold it accountable
for the result, as you hold me accountable for my
paramount obedience to the law of nature, issuing
perchance in drunkenness, perchance in theft.   Undoubtedly the ruin of the planet would ensue in that
case, but you would not charge this ruin upon the

planet itself, but upon the constitution of nature
which allowed its centrifugal or projectile impetus
to overcome its centripetal or attractive one. The
planet itself does not create these forces, but simply
obeys them. If, therefore, the one grow stronger
than the other, and sweep the planet to destruction,
and a suit be thereupon instituted for damages, it
seems to me that the heirs of the planet have the
exclusive right to the position of plaintiff, while the
general constitution of nature should occupy that
of defendant.

In like manner, I do not create the laws of my
finite self-consciousness, I merely obey them. As
Swedenborg has shown in a very complete manner,
neither charity nor self-love, neither moral good
nor moral evil, has its origin in the individual, but
only in good or bad association. All charity, he
says, is an influx into man from heavenly association; all self-love an influx into him from infernal
association. Hence he says, God never attributes
good nor evil to a man, never sees in him either
merit or demerit. In truth, he represents God as
wholly ignoring the moral man, the man who is
subject either to nature or society, either to hell or
heaven, and acknowledging only the Lord or perfect man, the man who subjects both hell and

heaven to his own individuality, and so ensures an unimpeded intercourse between the divine and human, between the Creator and creature.

If these things be true, and they cannot be denied save at the expense of rationality, and the proportionate advantage of brutality or materiality, then clearly I should not be held accountable for my moral delinquencies. If I obey the law of nature to excess—if I yield self-love a disproportionate homage—and if, at the same time, my subjection to this law is purely passive, depending not on my own will or foresight, but upon the countervailing power of another law, the law of society; then manifestly this excess or disproportion is not an attribute of my individuality, but only of society. Society is bound by the interests of my individuality, of which it is the guardian, not to allow nature an excessive grasp of my energies. If, then, nature exert this grasp, the blame attaches not to me, but to society, which fails to attract me to my kind as powerfully as nature contrives to seduce me away. To be sure, I suffer in this state of things, becoming perhaps a miserable sot or dexterous rogue, turning my individuality into a hideous distortion of the true divine image. But pity and not blame is what this lot demands, for it is one of suffering. I suffer. It is only society which sins in allowing me to suffer, that is, in so bedevilling and embittering my relations with my fellow-man, that I am necessarily driven to seek in nature a solace which nature is not empowered to yield.

This, I am profoundly convinced, is the attitude which it behooves every lover of God and man to assume towards our existing society, an attitude of utter contempt and defiance as to its justifying and condemning power. No other basis is to be found for the vileness which besets us, no foothold exists for our prevalent unrighteousness, but in the limitary self hood which society imposes on us. It is only because society denies me a consciousness of unity with God, by obstinately limiting my unity with nature and man, that I become tortured with this conscience of sin. Society, that arch-liar and hypocrite which continually seeks to justify itself by the defamation of its offspring, is my sole accuser before God. Destroy, therefore, the imperfections of our social institutions, or, what is the same thing, allow man's internal freedom a perfect outward development, and you instantly destroy all unrighteousness and all Pharisaic pride among men. In that event our mere relative or contingent good would give place to positive and universal good.

No man would then appear good by the contrast of another's evil, nor any appear evil by the contrast of another's good, but every man would be positively good, good by the manifest and unlimited indwelling of the divine power.

This is the last great triumph of humanity, the signal for the complete inauguration of God's kingdom on earth—the triumph of the individual over society. Let society give up its unhallowed and futile labor of exalting itself above man, and become as it should be purely subservient and tributary to him, then no man will incur the reproach of evil by an undue devotion to the law of his nature. By forgetting, as it now does, its intrinsic vanity, and exalting itself into a divine end, it not only corrupts and degrades man, but invites, nay solicits, the vengeance of God.

For there can be no more flagrant affront to the Divine Humanity, to God's end in creation, than for the moral life to regard itself as final. If I take my stand upon my moral attributes, upon the life I derive from my relations to my own body and my fellow-man, if I say on the one hand that there is no higher good, no good more positive for me, than that which stands in my fulfilment of these relations, and on the other no lower evil, no evil more positive for me, than that which stands in my neglect of these relations, I do, in reality, dwarf my destiny, and debar the divine communication to me. If I persuade myself or allow society to persuade me that God desires only my moral excellence, only my exemplary obedience to all my duties as husband and father, neighbor and citizen, I am under a profound misconception of the divine righteousness. What God wants is to see a *perfect* society among men, to see an *infinite* fellowship binding every man with every man, because this society or fellowship is a necessary means to the revelation of His own glory in man. But this perfect society, this infinite fellowship of man with man, is incessantly baulked by our moral differences, the differences engendered by our petty social institutions. It is impossible that any true fellowship or concord can subsist where one party is good and another evil, because the former feels a sense of merit, a sense of superior desert, which incessantly piques the jealousy of the other and so defeats every emotion of a tender and enduring friendship.

If we could be content with *being* good husbands, good parents, good neighbors and citizens; if we could refrain from indulging a secret chuckle of self-

complacency in these qualifications; if we could
refrain from viewing ourselves as inwardly superior on these accounts to publicans and harlots;
then no objection would lie, because then we should
not identify ourselves with society, nor drown our
vital force in the feculent mud of morality. Then
we should look upon all these relations as purely
provisional, as only so many advancing steps or
means to the realization of that perfect society
through which God would achieve the complete development and aggrandizement of every individual
soul, or secure His unimpeded communion with
every creature He has made.

But such is not the fact. We are not content to
fulfil these relations. We make their fulfilment a
ground of merit before God, a means of righteousness. For doing all these things we look upon ourselves as so much better than the man who stands
afar off, and has nothing but sins to reckon up before
God. Consequently, by just so much as we deem
ourselves already to possess, do we grow indifferent
to what God has in store for us. Thus society, by
looking upon its present attainments or institutions
as final, and teaching its subjects to esteem themselves righteous or unrighteous in God's sight as
they stand affected to these institutions, really de-

feats the divine righteousness, opposes the advent of the divine humanity, and keeps man in perpetual bondage to the beggarly elements of this world's knowledge. Forgetting its intrinsic stewardship or subordination, looking upon itself not as the servant of man but as his superior and affixing its foolish praise or foolish reproach to him as he obeys or disobeys its will, it snatches him from the hand of his Creator, defeats every access of the divine image in him, and reduces him oftentimes to a condition below the brute.

For all these things society avouches itself traitorous to God and the inevitable heir of his wrath. In this conflict there can be no paltering nor compromise on the part of God. He must by the very necessity of His perfection become the source of infinite ability and joy to every creature. If therefore any man or any society of men choose to take their stand upon their morality, upon any of those differences which separate them from other men and other societies, and say these things constitute God's true glory in man, constitute the true ground of hope and expectation towards Him, then God is bound to ally himself with the reverse aspect of humanity, is bound to declare Himself the friend of publicans and sinners rather then of these men, and to devise accordingly their utter and pitiless overthrow.

Thus it is not the moral life itself which is hurtful, but only the stupid pride and self-complacency with which we view our attainments in that direction. We become satisfied with ourselves as morally engendered, as morally distinguished from other men, and hence when the divine man presents himself in any forerunner or harbinger, he is so totally unlike ourselves that we see no beauty in him that we should covet him. Well said the Christ, "how hard is it for them that HAVE riches to enter the kingdom of heaven !" It is, in fact, easier for a camel to go through the eye of a needle than for a rich man to enter the kingdom of God. Why? Because the sole title to that kingdom lies in the all-giving and nought-exacting love of God, and therefore to suppose any previous qualification in the subject apposite to it, whether such qualification be natural or moral, is grossly to belie it.

But the evil is irremediable while society continues to interpose between man and God. So long as society declares itself final, looking upon man as made for it instead of itself as made for him, it must inevitably degrade him into a coxcomb or a slave. Representing his destiny as merely social

or relative because standing in his voluntary subjection to his fellow-man, instead of individual and
positive because standing in his spontaneous subjection to God, it teaches him to regard morality as
God's prime end in creation, and to expect His favor accordingly or dread His frown just as he
obeys or disobeys his social obligations. Thus it
turns the affluent fountain of my life into a pinched
and miserly task-master, making my hope towards
Him contingent upon a certain foregone good in myself rather than upon His own exuberant grace.
In thus sundering me from God, in thus removing
Him to such a freezing distance from me, it renders
me the prey of every cowardly imagination, of
every disgusting and diabolical superstition. For
it bids me, above all things, distrust my own spontaneous emotions, my own inward affections. As
it makes God wholly external to me, as it makes
Him remote from me by all its own breadth of in-
terposition between us, more remote from me than
any man, so it makes my inward emotions and affections further from Him even than my senses are,
and converts them into a proportionably fallacious
testimony concerning Him. Leading me thus to
distrust above all things my inward self, my private emotions and sympathies, it at the same time

and in exactly corresponding measure leads me to *trust the testimony of my senses*, and especially *the testimony of other men my elders*, and more especially still *the men who lived near the reputed birth of time*, and had, therefore, the most immediate news concerning Him.

Thus moralism is the parent of fetichism, or superstitious worship, the parent of all sensual and degrading ideas of God, the parent of all cruel and unclean and abominable worship. Leading me as it does to regard my inward self as corrupt, to distrust my heart's affections as the deadliest enmity to God, it logically prompts the crucifixion of those affections as especially well pleasing to Him, and bids me therefore offer my child to the flames, clothe my body in sackcloth and ashes, lacerate my skin, renounce the comforts and refinements of life, turn hermit or monk, forswear marriage, wear lugubrious and hideous dresses that insult God's daylight, and make myself, in short, under the guise of a voluntary and mendacious humility, perfectly ulcerous with spiritual pride, a mass of *living* purulence and putridity.

It is, I repeat, simply inevitable that moralism, or the doctrine of man's subjection to society, should produce these effects, should enormously inflame the pride of one class of its subjects, and as enormously depress that of another class. For if I, being a morally good man, that is, conscientiously abstaining from all injustice or injury to my neighbor, come to regard that character as constituting a distinction for me in the sight of God, as giving me a distinction there above some poor devil of an opposite character, it is easy to see that I must become as inwardly full of conceit and inhumanity as a nut is full of meat. How can it be otherwise? If the All-seeing behold in me any superiority to the most leprous wretch that defiles your streets, then clearly I have the highest sanction for esteeming myself above that wretch, and treating him not with fellow-feeling, but with condescension and scorn.

I know the unctuous cant, the shabby sophistry, which prevails upon this subject. I know it will be replied that I " ought not " forsooth! to do thus, that it " would be wrong " forsooth! for me to exalt myself above this poor wretch on the ground of my superior morality. But wherefore wrong? If that morality really distinguish me before God, if it constitute a superior claim to the divine favor, then it were flat inconsistency in me, it were flat treason to God not to acknowledge it in my practice. Can God's judgment be unrighteous? Wherefore then should I hesitate in any case to conform my conduct to it?

"Ah!" replies some one, "but *you* do no not see as God sees. If you saw all the temptations that have beset that poor wretch, if you could see, in the first place, the superior intensity of his passions to yours, his comparative intellectual disadvantages, his depraved circumstances from infancy up, and so forth, you would possibly regard your difference as small, and abate somewhat the tone of your triumph." This is all true. This is exactly what I myself say. But then if the circumstances here alleged should affect my judgment of my poor friend, much more should they affect *His* judgment to whom they are so much better known! If I cease on these grounds to exalt myself over my fellow, how much more must God cease to exalt me! But if this be so, what becomes of your moral distinctions in His sight? If He have no higher esteem for me, a morally good man, than He has for you, a morally evil man, then it is clear that the moral life is not the life He confers, the life about which He is chiefly solicitous.

You perceive that you are here in a dilemma. Either God esteems me a virtuous man above you a vicious man, or He does not. If He does, then inasmuch as all His judgments are right, and designed for our instruction, I should instantly learn to esteem myself above you, that is, to withhold from you sympathy or fellowship, in which case I become inhuman by virtue of a direct divine influence. If, on the other hand, He do not esteem me a virtuous man, above you a vicious man, then you deny the moral life to be God's life in man.

How will you extricate yourself from this dilemma? There is but one way. You will say that it was not your intention to represent God as holding one man intrinsically superior, or superior in himself, to another, but relatively or socially superior only; superior, that is, with reference to the purposes of society. There is consequently no further quarrel between us. Moral distinctions belong purely to our earthly genesis and history. They do not attach to us as the creatures of God. As the creature of society, I am either good or evil. I am good as keeping my natural gratification within the limits of social prescription, or evil as allowing it to transcend those limits. But as the creature of God, or in my most vital and final selfhood, I am positively good; good without any oppugnancy of evil; good, not by any stinted angelic mediation, but by the direct and unstinted indwelling of the Godhead.

I have now expressed my thought with more
detail than befits a popular Lecture.   But as I conceive the subject to be of especial interest to all
thoughtful minds, I am anxious to commend it to
your perfect apprehension.   With this view, let me
still further ask your indulgent attention, while I
discuss an objection which may possibly arise in
the minds of some of my audience.

It was alleged, on the delivery of the preceding
Lecture, that I deny moral distinctions.   The allegation is vaguely worded, but is doubtless worthy
of respectful investigation.   If it mean, then, that I
deny any difference between good and evil actions ;
that I call murder, adultery, theft, and so forth,
good actions ; of course the charge is silly and not
worth refuting.   In this sense no man ever denied
moral distinctions.   No man—not even the unfortunate subject of them—ever justified adultery,
theft, murder, or falsehood.   No man ever did one
of these things spontaneously, or at the instance of
his taste.   I have indeed heard of persons who had
a *mania* for theft ; who, from some exceptional
cerebral organization, could omit no opportunity to
enrich themselves at the expense of others.   But
these cases are regarded, of course, as exceptions
to the ordinary tenor of human nature, and as

putting the subject beyond the pale of responsibility. Because, if there be a constitutional aptitude to this offence in the party, you manifestly acquit the party himself of it. You would no more hold him personally responsible under these circumstances, than you would hold him personally liable for a hare-lip or any other morbid development. No man, then, I repeat, ever injured another from taste or spontaneity. Hence no man ever justified a moral delinquency, ever supposed himself acting worthily in taking his neighbor's life, property, or good name, or in seducing the affections of his wife.

The objector consequently does not mean to say that I confound good and evil actions, since the constitution of the human mind makes that impossible.

He means then, doubtless, that I do not regard the man who does good actions as intrinsically better than the man who does evil actions. He means, doubtless, that I do not regard the morally good man as possessing any superior claims upon the divine favor to the morally evil man, but view them both as heirs of the same eventual and glorious destiny. If the objector means this by his charge, then let me suggest an amendment of its form. Let him say to me: you deny, not the existence or importance of moral distinctions among men, but simply their divinity. You deny that God is in any measure privy to these distinctions.

To the charge, thus amended, I freely plead guilty. I am persuaded that God's eyes, however universal their empire, have never yet been astounded by the appearance of evil in His creatures. Whence should that evil come? It cannot come from Himself, who is essential good. Whence, then, should it have come? For the supposition, you perceive, makes it a phenomenon of God's creation; it is the possibility of evil in God's creature that we are discussing. How could evil be possible in that creature? You may say that it came from the Devil. Very well; let that answer stand.

If evil came from the Devil, then the Devil in infusing evil into God's creature acted either with God's consent or without it. If he acted with it, then of course God saw that it would not injure the creature, since He had methods of turning it all to the creature's superior profit, and so proving the Devil a fool for his pains. If he acted without God's consent, then of course you give the Devil not only a superior power to God, but a superior power over God's own work, or in the sphere of God's own activity. That is to say, you make the absolute creature of infinite Good confess himself the offspring of a deeper paternity—the paternity of infinite Evil.

But take either branch you choose of this hideous dilemma, you manifestly absolve the creature himself of all defilement. For whether the Devil infuse evil into him with or without the consent of Deity, it is clearly an operation under which the creature himself is passive, and I fancy that even the Devil is too good a logician to hold one responsible for his passions, but only for his actions. Any child might otherwise refute him. My passional nature means my various susceptibility of enjoyment and suffering from nature and man; my passions are merely the concrete forms of this various susceptibility. You would not therefore hold me responsible for my passions, unless you at the same time ascribed to me the paternity of nature and man—unless you at the same time held me to have created this universal frame of nature and society to which these passions owe all their existence.

Thus the Devil turns out an unprofitable hypothesis. He is an infinite lie. No one can trust in him without being confounded. He looms portentously large in all infant cosmologies—in all those theories of creation which are constructed by the

sensuous imagination of the race; but you have
only to prick him with the smallest pin of science,
and he fairly roars you a confession of egregious
imbecility.

The entire traditional doctrine of the origin of
evil is irrational and abhorrent. In one phasis it
asperses the divine goodness; in another the divine
power. One hypothesis represents God as allowing
evil to appear in the creature only that He might
display His sovereignty, not in reconciling it with
good and so affording a basis for His own adequate
manifestation in nature, but in afflicting it with
ceaseless torments. Surely this is a puerile conception of God which makes him capable of ostentation, capable of enjoying a mere empty parade of
His power. The conception converts Him, in fact,
into an aggravated bully, intent upon the display of
his physical prowess. It is grovelling and disgusting beyond every other product of our sensuous imagination. It degrades Deity below the brute even.
For the tiger makes no sacrifice to ostentation. He
inflicts no suffering in demonstration of his power
and the consequent gratification of his vanity, but
only in satisfaction of an honest natural appetite.
If accordingly, this hypothesis of creation were
just, moral distinctions would be seen to claim a

basis in God's want of love, in His inferiority to tigers.

The other hypothesis attributes evil to a defect, not of the divine goodness, but of the divine power. It represents God as designing to make man morally good. But as moral good is in its very nature finite or conditional, as it is conditioned upon the inseparable coexistence of moral evil, so God, however much He may desire it, is practically unable to keep evil out of the universe. From the nature of the case, from the nature of the good He designs to bestow, He cannot make one man good without making another evil. Hence you perceive that evil stalks into creation in spite of God, being involved in the good He would create. The only way, consequently, in which He might exclude it, would be to forego His creative design altogether. For His design being to create moral good, and moral good standing in the inseparable antagonism of moral evil, in effect or practically His design is to create the one as much as the other.

We may, indeed, represent the evil man as so much inevitable chips, or waste material; but we gain nothing by this motion. For is not he always esteemed an imperfect workman who leaves chips behind him, who cannot work without a shocking waste of material? Our divines see fit, indeed, to blink all these monstrous contradictions, and doubtless they have a reward. But is it not gratuitous in them to go further than this, and represent the Deity not merely as making chips, but also as vindictively bestowing an everlasting vitality on these chips in order to their never-ending combustion?

According to this hypothesis, then, you perceive that moral distinctions among men grow out of a defect in the divine power. The former hypothesis attributes them to a defect of God's goodness, or an inferiority of His internal endowments. The latter attributes them to a defect of his power or an inferiority of his external endowments. Each proceeds upon an implication of His imperfection, and hence they are both alike intrinsically absurd and blasphemous.

Such is the inevitable effect of making God " a respecter of persons." If you make His life moral, if you make it to stand in the antagonism of evil, you necessarily finite or degrade Him, and render every exertion of His power essentially violent and disorderly. I marvel that the coincidence of revelation with reason on this subject has not attracted more attention. For the very opening page of the Bible, relates that when Adam under the tuition of the sensual principle, symbolized by the serpent, came to the knowledge of good and evil, or the experience of morality, he instantly found himself excluded from the participation of the divine life.

No, my friends, we may rest assured that this life depends upon no paltry distinctions of good and evil among its subjects. These distinctions prove only our destitution of it. They spring not from God, but from our ignorance and inexperience of God. They spring out of the ignorance which society is under of its own subordinate relation to man, and the consequently futile efforts it makes to justify itself at his expense. Our social forms or institutions being so partial, so limitary, so imperfect as they necessarily must be in the infancy of human culture, they do not immediately justify themselves to our regard, but on the contrary exact a large body of persons to conserve and administer them. This class of persons accordingly, because they perform such eminent public uses, soon come to enjoy distinguished honor, wealth, and power; soon come, in fact, to be identified with society, and to isolate its interests from those of the mass of individual members. The unrighteous division thus made between society and the individual, between the public and private interest of man, is the great evil under which humanity groans, and with which God's providence has to contend. For these persons, the ruling and propertied classes who are thus identified with society, forever keep it from advancing with the advance of the individual genius. They make their own wants the measure of the wants of society—of humanity. While they can clothe themselves in purple and fine linen and fare sumptuously every day they think the interests of society sufficiently secured, and have no eye for the sores of the great Lazarus of humanity who lies outside of their gates. Hence these people incessantly dwarf our social structure; incessantly prevent its keeping pace with the individual life; at all events, they are sure to make no concession to the individual demand so long as resistance to that demand consists with the stability of their usurpation.

Society must therefore make haste to shed this parasitic life, and reconcile itself with universal humanity. Let it give over the ungodly labor of exalting itself above man, of subjecting the individual dignity to its tyrannous sway, and all its disorders will instantly cease. So long as it pretends to a paramount place in God's regard; so long as it believes that God cares for it first and for man secondly, and therefore strives to compel man's spirit into its allegiance, the whole sweep and torrent of God's majestic life becomes its enemy—becomes pledged to subvert its power and trail its glory in the dust.

Society may enact its foolish revenges. It may paint humanity never so blackly. It may persist in stifling man's passional freedom, and whenever the sufferer re-acts by God's deathless force within him against this compression, it may variously name him liar, murderer, thief, adulterer; may confiscate his goods, degrade his family, immure him in prison, and finally quench the life in his manly bosom. But God is not mocked. For all these things the grand final reckoning comes on apace. Every drop of criminal blood which society first brews and then pours out upon the ground, springs up an armed hand to continue the quarrel, until at last society becomes actually beggared by her own pauper and criminal progeny, until at last, as is the case with England at present, society has actually no room to bestow her paupers and criminals in, and wanders the wide world over begging the hospitality of affrighted islands.

Be assured then, my friends, that crime will grow, that human life and every human possession will continue to decline in value, until society wakes from her dismal delusion, and confesses herself the obedient steward to man. When she confesses herself no longer the sovereign, but the servant of every man, woman, and child within her borders; when accordingly she no longer seeks to restrain, much less to extirpate, the God-given passions of humanity, but how she may best promote their free and *therefore* orderly action ; then, and not till then, will crime and vice cease throughout the earth, then and not till then will every man sit under his own vine and fig-tree with none to molest or make him afraid.

But enormous as this Lecture has grown, I still cannot afford to close it without a few words more of practical illustration.

You have all been shocked by the news of the recent horrid murder in Boston. I need not recite the disgusting particulars. The injury to the victim himself is small, moreover, when compared with that inflicted on his family and dependents, and especially on the family and friends of the criminal, whomsoever he may prove to be.

I have no opinion, and therefore express none, as to the guilt or innocence of the person actually charged with this hideous outrage. But I wish you for a moment to suppose him guilty, to take for granted that the murder was perpetrated by him under the circumstances and with the provocation popularly alleged. And now, having done this, I beg you to notice two facts.

First, you will observe that the crime grew out of a money-relation between the parties. Professor WEBSTER having placed himself under pecuniary obligation to Dr. PARKMAN, and failing to meet that obligation, had incurred a suspicion of dishonesty in the mind of the creditor. The smart of this suspicion is said to have been aggravated by the creditor's private inquiries and insinuations as to the responsibility of the debtor, who thereupon, it is presumed, moved both by an inability to cancel the obligation and by an overpowering sense of insult and oppression, seized an opportune moment and dealt his creditor a treacherous and revolting death.

Manifestly, then, this crime grew out of a purely social relation between the parties—the relation of debtor and creditor. Had society refused to authorize this relation by giving every man independence of his neighbor, the crime would never have been committed. It springs not out of any original or innate hatred in one human bosom towards another; but strictly out of a false social relation between the parties—a relation which makes every man more or less dependent for the means of his own subsistence upon the infirm will of his brother. In strict truth, therefore, society itself is guilty of this outrage. No one claims that Prof. WEBSTER has any native taste for murder, that he would rather murder men than not murder them. If, then, he exhibit no *a priori* preference or taste for this mode of action, it is clear that his action must have been constrained—constrained by the vicious relations which society organized between him and his unfortunate victim.

In the second place, you will observe the fact of Prof. WEBSTER's past good repute. He had borne an unblemished character till this event. I believe that he had suffered pecuniary embarrassments, but it is reported of him that he was an affectionate husband and father, a faithful friend, given to elegant hospitality, an enthusiastic promoter of science and the fine arts, especially music, a kind neighbor, and an orderly citizen.

Now, my friends, observe the stupidity of our social methods. In killing this man for the offence imputed and proved, society does not kill the murderer merely; it kills the tender husband and father as well, it kills the friend of humane science, the friend of the beautiful arts, the hospitable neighbor, the orderly citizen. It blinks out of sight these life-long characteristics of the subject, and, for one deed of transient frenzy, brands him with the abhorred name of murderer. But good God! can this be justice? Does God bid us, in killing the murderer, kill also the upright citizen, the man who is estimable in all relations, not by fits and starts, nor by strenuous efforts, but in the continuous tenor of his life? No; let Him be true and every man a liar rather.

God has no enmity to the good husband and parent, the good friend and neighbor. His enmity burns only towards the murderer, the thief, the liar, the adulterer; these he delivers over to an irrevocable contempt, to an everlasting damnation. They are by their very nature evanescent existences, and shall never partake of his eternity. Let society therefore take heed to itself how it exacts the penalty of its violated bond! It deals with a subtler judge than Shylock found in Portia, and one far more inexorable to after pleas. If it shed one drop of innocent blood, if, in punishing the murderer, thief, or adulterer, it harm to the extent of one hair the man made in God's image, let it be sure that His vengeance will not tarry. Let it be very sure that He only waits a fitting moment to break it asunder and scatter it like the stubble that passeth away by the wind of the wilderness.

Rely upon it, that God loves man and hates only those things which defile and obscure him; hates, that is, all those characters like the murderer and so forth, which humanity disowns and which belong therefore exclusively to an immature society, to an imperfectly-organized fellowship among men. These characters have no inherent vitality, have only a transient individuality. They do not attach to humanity like the poet or musician; they are a remnant of the animal nature imprisoned in our social institutions, and not quite refined into the human. It is society alone which perpetuates these brutal relations between man and man, relations of force, of obligatory courtesy, which keep us forever incredulous of any spontaneous and lasting harmony.

The perfect man at his coming will banish these inhuman characters from his presence forever, will shut them up to everlasting destruction. How? *By reforming the relations which now generate them*, by re-organizing society upon the methods of science, methods which shall completely reconcile interest and duty, self-love and charity. By putting away these vicious relations and introducing better ones in their stead, he, of course, excludes all the ills which legitimately issue from them. Thus he visits the murderer, thief, adulterer, and so forth, with everlasting destruction, while, at the same time, he saves with an everlasting salvation the noble and friendly soul which so long lay obscured under these conditions.

You perhaps think it a fair objection to this assertion of man's essential innocence, that the criminal does not always hasten to confess his actual guilt, that he oftentimes refuses to confess it when a possible mitigation of punishment might ensue. But the circumstance thus objected really confirms the assertion, for it constitutes merely the form of the criminal's protest against the injustice of society. Every man instinctively affirms his essential innocence, affirms that crime is a pure imposition of his social relations. He feels in his inmost soul that he is unimplicated in the abominable deeds of his body, unimplicated in the exact measure of their abomination. He feels that he himself is inwardly good and amiable and worthy, even while these things were committed. If therefore society in dealing with the criminal would observe this law of consciousness, if it would say to him not " you yourself are evil and detestable and worthy therefore to be hunted

down and killed like any wild beast," but only
"your deeds are evil and detestable, and to be put
a stop to therefore at all hazards, even to the taking
of your life," there is no criminal who would not
accept the verdict and joyfully give his life a ransom
for his soul.

But society has hitherto been incapable of this
wisdom. It seeks to falsify the verdict of the individual consciousness, and to prove not merely the
deed, but him the doer also, evil. It says to him,
"you have not merely done an evil deed, but you
yourself are an evil man, different from the honorable men who judge you, and we shall therefore
kill you out of our midst like any atrocious vermin,
and your name shall be an infamy to all that derive
it from you." God's truth is pledged to sustain a
man under such infernal calumny as this. Every
soul of man resents it by a deathless divine instinct,
by the instinct of a righteousness never perhaps realized till it becomes so loudly demanded.

Accordingly, rather than confess under these circumstances that he did the deed, rather than confess by confessing it that he is the miserable rep-
tile society paints him, the criminal keeps his own
steadfast counsel, dies as we say and makes no
sign. But this signless death, my friends, is a fear-

ful sign for society. When that poor wretch stands arrayed in hood and shroud under your unmelting eyes, when society resolves itself into a bestial mob to embitter the last moments of a life which it alone has desecrated, when the pale and manly victim defies your Pharisaic rage and dies as he lived despising your hollow righteousness, then you may indeed cry out, " Behold how the enemies of society perish ;" but in my heart of hearts I believe that you are all the while stupidly provoking the enmity of an imperishable enemy, even God. all truth and goodness. There is no lie so damnable in His sight as that of man's essential depravity, because there is none so subversive of His own honor. Until this lie be disavowed by society therefore, organically disavowed ; until society, by putting away its present unequal methods, assume all guilt to itself and justify every soul of man ; God will continue its enemy. The things which are highly esteemed of it, its priests and rulers, He will count an abomination ; and those whom it makes last, its felons, its slaves, its harlots, He will make first, ministering to them a joyful and abundant entrance to His kingdom.

Now, my friends, suppose for a moment that society should become aroused from its unbelief and

obedient to these benign ideas, so reverential towards
God, so full of benefaction to man. Do you think
that the practical results would be bad? Let us see.

Suppose that society, animated by these truths,
should go to the criminal whom we suppose to have
been convicted of murder, and address him thus:
"Friend, we have erred, and have come to recall our
error. We are convinced that the odium of murder
does not attach to your soul. We are convinced
that you would never have felt a prompting to injure him who now lies dead had we previously done
our duty towards you, that is, had we previously
insured you both that ample supply of all your
natural and social wants, which it is alike our interest and duty to ensure all our members, and
which would have forever prevented either of you
falling under the other's obligation. Failing thus in
our duty, we have tempted you to mutual rapacity
and injury. One of you lies low, hurried out of nature in the midst of health and joy; to him it is too
late to make amends. But to you, the less happy
survivor, we can at least do justice, by assuming
the odium of your guilt. We are the really guilty
party. The inhuman relations we have organized
between you pronounce us the criminal. Are we
not accordingly suffering the award due to crime in

those innocent yet bleeding hearts more intimately connected with the deceased and yourself? Wherefore we do not condemn *thee;* go and sin no more."

Now, my friends, do you conceive that if society should act with this magnanimity, with this truth, the criminal would not melt into instant tenderness? Would he not at once cry out to this beneficent society—" my life, my all shall be yours. It was not the suffering that I dreaded, it was not my approaching violent doom that I contended against. It was the stigma you cast upon my private soul that outraged me, the feeling tqat I was to suffer unblest of God, unblest of man, unblest even of that noble and tender wife whom my deed has disgraced, and of those fond confiding children I have so patiently reared to manhood. This was the wormwood and the gall, that I should die and no man say, God bless you, die abhorred of my own flesh and blood. But your magnanimity restores me to myself. It justifies my inmost loathing and abhorrence of this guilt, and restores me to self-respect, restores me to God. For whoso is at peace with his own heart is at peace with God. Take therefore the life you have given. Use it freely, to its last gasp if occasion serve. Can a man value his body when he possesses himself in God? Try me and see. Reconciled to myself, reconciled to God, rejoicing by your truth in a soul washed clean from all defilement, rejoicing for the first time in virgin innocence of soul, I abandon this bleak existence to your service as freely as ever saint upon the verge of the beatific vision abandoned himself to God."

DATE DUE

DEC 29 1992			